ROAD BIKE RACING & PREPARATION

ROAD BIKE RACING
& PREPARATION

RAY KNIGHT

OSPREY

Published in 1989 by Osprey Publishing Limited
59 Grosvenor Street, London W1X 9DA

British Library Cataloguing in Publication Data

Knight, Ray
    Road Bike Racing and Preparation.
    1. Racing motorcycles. Racing
    I, Title
    796.7'2
ISBN 0–85045–807–2

Printed and bound in Great Britain by
Butler & Tanner Ltd, Frome and London

Contents

Introduction

Motorcycle racing today is increasingly based upon road bikes and never before have there been more opportunities to take part in the action.

Now, there are championship series at club and national level for bikes that you can buy straight off the showroom floor (production), and others for modified machines, Superstock, Seniorstock and Juniorstock. At whatever level you might choose to make your debut on the tarmac, the opportunities are wider than they have ever been.

For the motorcycle enthusiast with a taste for speed, racing offers a supreme chance to join the select band of those who participate rather than just watch from the sidelines. The chance to be part of a scene that is at once intensely competitive and yet comprised of like-minded enthusiasts that will help you to get on to the grid, if you need it, and race you to the flag, generates a camaraderie that surely has little equal.

You can choose to use your road bike almost as it leaves the showroom floor, or modify it for more performance if you wish. Other classes give you the choice of an inexpensive start with a machine that you can build up yourself or perhaps by buying a model already used for racing.

However, even if you choose the easy route with

the bike 'as you buy', there are still a number of things you will have to do to prepare the machine for competing. This will not be tuning in any sense of the word, it will be preparation that *must* be carried out before the bike will be allowed on the grid.

Whichever route into racing you choose, this book will guide you through the maze of regulations and procedures you have to undergo before you can take your place on the grid. It gives guidelines on what it will cost, analyses the attributes of a successful racer and suggests how to identify short-comings and compensate for them.

In short, this book will enable you to avoid the many possible pitfalls when making your racing debut, and make the most of your chances when you do.

Ray Knight

Above left **Motorcycle racing need not mean two wheels only. Classic sidecar racing is exciting and affordable**

Below left **Geoff Fowler pilots the** *Motor Cycle News* **Yamaha FZ 750 as part of the team contesting the Coupe de Endurance Championship in 1987**

Right **The tops at the time – the British champion, Roger Marshall, aboard the Honda Britain works machine in the 1986 TT**

About the author

Ray has been a successful motorcycle racing competitor and journalist for over a generation and in this book analyses what makes a successful road racer and advises on how to get into the sport.

From a career that started at Silverstone in 1958 Ray has raced on tracks all over the world and is still competing both at endurance grand prix level and club events. With club lap records to his credit on several circuits and many championships won, Ray is an Isle of Man TT Production race winner, having competed in over 70 races and collected 17 Replicas. In 1988 he achieved a lap time of over 109 mph on the TT course and has completed over 25,000 miles on the track.

Works machinery has featured in his career and as long ago as 1973 he rode a Norton in the Le Mans 24 Hours race. Other marques have included Triumph, Ducati, Royal Enfield and BMW.

Recent successes were winning the 1987 Pirelli Six Hours Production Championship round, in the 750 cc class, at Brands Hatch, and the Newmarket Production and British Formula 1300 Championships.

His current machine is a Suzuki GSX-R 1100 which he prepares himself and he is currently sponsored by *Motorcycle Sport* magazine, Centurion Helmets, Shell, Pirelli Tyres, Ferodo, Manx Leathers and John Harris Motorcycles. During 1987 he rode in the World Endurance Championship with Team Chell Instruments. He carries out racing machine tests for *Motorcycle Sport*.

In a racing career that spans 30 years and from Triumphs to the latest Suzuki 1100, Ray Knight puts all that experience into this book for the benefit of those just starting out to enjoy a great experience

Above Competing in the World Endurance Championship in the Bol d'Or 24 Hours in 1986. The author aboard Team Centaur's GSX-R Suzuki

Left Ray Knight on a Triumph in the 1973 500 Production TT. One of these could just be persuaded to do a genuine 120 mph. It used to be possible to modify a production bike out of all recognition according to the rules at the time

1

What makes a racer?

Some champions are born, others have sufficient dedication and determination to become champions. Many will race for the sheer fun and glory of it while achieving more modest goals.

I doubt if I could have numbered among the top runners even with all the breaks, but with hindsight I could have exploited my talent and meagre resources to greater effect given the experience of more than 30 years of competition behind me. This experience should help the newcomer get started in competitive racing more easily and more quickly than I was able to in the 1950s.

Over three decades of road racing have given me enormous fun and also a fair idea of what questions I'd have asked if I were starting all over again, if only I could turn the clock back. So what I have attempted to do is to analyse the qualities of a successful racer, to guide your thoughts more positively towards competing, and perhaps to give an appreciation of what goes on in the minds of the guys out there, up front.

Racing requires much more than that touch of the tiger, it requires the will to win. You need a variety of attributes to temper and sustain the basic drive and to convert your thinking, actions and reactions into that of a professional racer. When I use the word professional I mean the approach and attitude to the sport, an attitude that will enable you to make the most of the qualities you have, and to minimize the disadvantages of those that count against you.

Racing is the ultimate ego trip. Each time you go out on to the grid, you are, if you think about it,

Roger Burnett being asked for his view after yet another of the race wins that earned him a place on the grand prix scene with Honda

challenging the rest of the riders to try and beat you. When you do win against, perhaps, some 39 other riders, then the moment is yours and you become hooked.

This is the good bit, but the subject for this chapter is, are you a potential champion? Have you the attributes, mental and physical, to get you to the front of the pack? Do you have the courage, dedication, skill and judgement and the killer instinct? Do you have in your make-up all the qualities of success?

It has to be said that I did not have many of them when making my debut on the club circuit at Silverstone in 1958. What is more, I didn't develop what I had, but through perseverance, I managed to win my first race after trying for seven years, going on to win a TT race in the Isle of Man and many club championships.

I took up racing in the first instance just for fun, to see what it was like. There aren't many Wayne Gardners, Eddie Lawsons or Mike Hailwoods about, maybe they were born to win. But if you

have sufficient determination to want to test your ability out there against the rest, anything is possible – you could be a winner.

The killer instinct

Some people are content just to take part in a race, others would not want to race unless they felt they had a chance of winning. Many continue to race without much success but keep the thought firmly in their minds that if only their bike was as fast as that of the winner, then they themselves might win one day. In their hearts, they might admit to doubts but we all have our illusions, indeed have to, to enable us to carry on. One thing's for sure, if you do race, you'll find out just how much of the killer instinct you have in your make-up.

However much dedication you may have, all will be in vain if you cannot take the calculated risk that sorts the men from the boys. It's not just a case of riding on your limit, feeding in the power until the seat of your pants informs you that another tenth of a 'thou' strain on the throttle wire and you're into a lurid rear-wheel slide, or of braking that couple of shuddering feet later, it's more.

In the hurly-burly of short circuit racing, races tend to be of the order of six laps, even shorter, so that missing the smallest opportunity to pass can mean the chance of losing a race. In the ballot for grid positions before a race, drawing the last rows can mean that when the action starts all you can see from your place at the back is a mass of weaving, jockeying machinery with seemingly little chance of

Below right **Niall McKenzie and Alan Carter scrap, note the slick tyres which are required to compete at national and international level. They are not allowed for club events**

Below **Some of the fruits of victory of a relatively successful racer; trophies from club, national and international races. These make it all seem worthwhile**

finding a way through before the first corner.

The chances are that you will be in that position many times throughout your first season and unless you are prepared to chance your arm to some extent and go for it into the middle and find a way through, you will still have the best part of the field in front of you going into the first bend, and the last one too. That means that the fast rider who started from the front of the grid has got a flyer and is half-way down the straight before you can even begin to get him into your sights. If he was one of the potential winners, you can forget that race for sure.

The killer instinct, or perhaps too much of it, will surely get you into trouble some day. If lots of bottle is all you've got, then you're potentially heading for an accident. A little ability helps too but for many it is just learning to gradually push back your own personal frontiers when you think that you are already on the limit. It's the need to catch the one in front that is the impetus the killer instinct provides but it needs to be tamed with gradually acquired experience.

If you have the killer instinct it will be the driving force at the start of the race when the lights change. Obvious? Not quite as much as you might think. The killer will have his motor running a fraction before the others, head on the tank while others are still getting the show on the road. He's the one that seldom hesitates when it comes to passing a slower rider coming into a corner. You'll be able to tell just by watching, since the attitude on the machine expresses determination. And he's usually got a few trophies on the sideboard to prove it.

Above all, the successful racer will be quick enough to seize the slightest opportunity, yet cool enough not to be led into a situation where disaster is the only conclusion. He will also be calculating enough in the heat of a race to plot and plan the overtaking move at the point where the opponent has no chance of coming back. For example, imagine following an almost evenly matched rival round for several laps until you spot the one corner where an opportunity could be grasped to get ahead, then deciding where he may be faster than you and sticking behind until the last lap for the bid for the lead. Trying earlier would let him know where you have an advantage that could be remedied next time round with an extra effort.

The killer is the man who, even with a slower machine, will get near enough to the leader to stay in his slipstream down the straight and will then continually show a front wheel to the leader pressurizing him into a mistake.

Another example that a winner may employ is to bluff braking distance when being chased hard. He may brake just a shade early each time at the end of a straight, allowing the pursuer to believe that he can make a last lap attempt to get by. When that last lap comes up though, the winner will brake right on the limit while the pursuer is lured into braking too late and running wide. Killer technique yes, but again tempered with reason.

Quick reactions

Faster than light reactions might well be thought of as the one vital necessity above all others for the successful racer. Certainly they are a pretty useful attribute and the ability to react quickly enough to spot that split second situation where advantage might be gained, or spot disaster a second before it occurs, while in the middle of a hard dice in a group, makes the winner. But all is not lost even if you are average.

In fact you could even have reasonably slow reactions and still make the fastest lap in the race and even win it. How? Above all, it is the most accurate judgement of speed, estimating distances, braking-points, of finding the best line through a corner and being able to ride at the limit of tyre adhesion, that enables the winner to circulate faster than the rest.

If, for instance, you do get into a slide, fast reactions may well enable you to react quickly enough to get you out of trouble, but nevertheless races certainly can be won without razor sharp reflexes. If you happen to be at the front, it's your riding ability comprising many of the attributes covered already that will get you round and staying ahead of the field. However, while they aren't an absolute necessity you'd undoubtedly be better with them than without.

Mechanical ability

There are successful racers who have won championships and yet lack any great mechanical competence. However, they to tend to be exceptions simply because unless you happen to have a mechanic willing and able to service your machine for you, then inevitably there are some jobs that cannot be avoided. It may simply be changing the gearing as you go to different circuits, swapping the odd spark plug or fitting new brake pads.

There is, however, rather more to it than just manipulating spanners. The rider with a rapport with his machine will sense when it is going at its best, conversely, he will intuitively know when something is amiss instead of just trying to drive it harder. By sensing when disaster is about to strike, a sensitive rider will save many an expensive repair bill. It can also enable a failing machine to be nursed to the finish to win the day. Or, by diagnosing trouble the problem can be quickly rectified as soon as you get back to the pits, in time to get out for the next race.

Good examples of riders with a mechanical sympathy with their machine are Joey Dunlop and Ron Haslam who can make an engine last a season and extract all the performance from it without over-stressing it. Others seem to suffer blowups with amazing regularity, though they are fast riders.

Close quarters

Perhaps the biggest single difference between riding fast on the road and racing, is simply that once you are out there on the track you will find many others at arm's length away from you, or closer. It can come as something of a surprise if you are not expecting it and while hardened scratchers are used to touching elbows or rubbing fairings, this can be quite a culture shock for the novice.

If that short statement does not sound particularly off-putting then neither should it, because dicing at close quarters is really the essence of the whole business and there is nothing else quite like the thrill of the cut and thrust of a close dice.

Having said that, we all have our own built-in limits acquired during the conditioning of everyday life. The racetrack is certainly not for the faint-hearted but then everything is relative. What may have been taking it easy for 'Fast Freddie Spencer' would be beyond the ability of most, which is why he became a legend in his own time, winning both the 250 and 500 cc World Championships in one

year; something practically everybody thought impossible when he announced his intention of competing in both classes.

Dedication

Once you start racing, no effort seems too much and no sacrifice too great to get yourself and the bike to the circuit for the next race. The shared hardships are part of the fun and a camaraderie develops out of a common purpose not shared by ordinary mortals on the outside of the spectator fences.

If you join the scene you will be on the road at sun-up on most weekends when the rest of the world is still between the sheets. Inevitably it seems, the tracks that you want to race at will be miles away. This usually requires leaving work as soon as you are able, loading the van or car and trailer and heading for the circuit that night. Then it may mean sleeping at the circuit in a tent or the back of the van, but the recompense can be sitting around a shared meal in the paddock over a beer with a crowd when exploits are recounted.

It means becoming so hooked on racing that you change your way of life, because in this sport there are no half measures. Riding once a month when it can be done comfortably and conveniently is not likely to hone your competitive abilities to any fine edge, and if you do have real ambitions, it will not

This is how close you will learn to ride when you trust your fellow competitors – no quarter asked or given as Alan Carter and Andy Watts duel

be enough to satisfy you in any case.

It will certainly mean spending most evenings of the season from March to October working on the bike, because there always seems to be something to check or change, or just giving the bike a good clean. 'Telly' watching will inevitably become a thing of the past as will many other pastimes, simply because racing is so time-consuming and absorbing. It's likely to demand most of your spare cash too. But more of that in the next chapter.

Don't despair

Having dwelt for so long on the desirable attributes of the successful racer it shouldn't be felt that because you feel that you may lack in possessing some, or even most, of them that racing would be a waste of time for you.

It is usually the case that once deficiencies are identified, you can be half-way towards compensating for them. A naturally fast rider will automatically and correctly estimate a braking-point for a corner – well to 95 per cent of what is possible anyway. It may be that your particular failing is in this very area and you find yourself being outbraked time after time, or perhaps when you try too hard, you continually run out wide, even off the track. It is here that a little planning, analysis and a scientific approach can pay off to the point of removing this particular deficiency from your list of reasons why you are not world championship material.

The approach to the problem is to identify some sort of marker at the trackside to aid your judgement in estimating when to brake on the approach to a corner. At many permanent tracks there are marker boards indicating the distance in yards before a corner. Failing something as obvious as braking at, say, the 200-yard signboard, maybe there is a subtle feature than can be picked out. For instance, a discolouration in the track surface itself, even a tuft of grass. Anything to give you a point of reference to gauge that last possible point at which to brake.

Try watching races to see if you can spot exactly where the fast men brake at any one corner. Identify it against some sort of marker and then gradually see if you can work up to the same point. Before trying it though, do make sure the rider you have watched is riding a machine with similar performance potential.

Perhaps the greatest advantage that this sort of

scientific approach to your racing can confer is consistency. A consistent rider is a safe one. Not just that but once having worked up to something like an optimum performance of his particular machine on a given track, he will always be fast on that track. The methodical approach to racing can turn a less talented rider into quite a competitive one against the many speedy but mercurial types who may win one day, crash the next and never quite succeed long enough to establish themselves.

Line ahead at Thruxton on the first lap. Races are
won or lost on making a good start. The riders at
the back of the picture really have their work cut
out but there are already another 20 or so behind
them

2

The costs of racing

Can you afford to go racing? The answer is probably yes, since you will no doubt already have a roadster of some sort and if you use it, then at least you do not have to buy a racing machine. This will, at the very least, give you the chance to try your hand to see if you are going to like it. If you are really pushed and are prepared to accept the obvious risk you could always ride your bike to the meeting, thereby avoiding the cost of transportation as well. If this does not appeal, your biggest expense will be the cost of buying a bike specifically for racing (see Chapter 4). It depends on how ambitious you choose to be. You could choose to race a BSA Bantam, an MZ or single-cylinder machine, in which case costs are fairly modest. Likewise, an old British classic bike could prove relatively inexpensive, though buying one of the latest 'remanufactured' Matchless G50s could cost more than most.

However, there are actually more obvious costs involved, simply in entering a meeting. A fee is payable for each race depending on the circuit. For example, it could range from £20 for one race on the short circuit at Brands Hatch in 1988, for eight to ten laps, to £75 for an entry in the Manx Grand Prix (however, this price would include a week's practice and the race, which covers over 37 miles of road per lap).

Costs are not so high away from the south and club meetings in the Midlands can be half the price, though if you are to travel all the way to a meeting, the chances are that you will want several rides to make the day worthwhile. You'll probably enter as many races as you can afford.

Transportation costs can quite easily be the biggest expense, but again it depends on how deep in the red you are prepared to go, as always it's a trade-off between your aspirations and how friendly you can get with your local bank manager.

A visit to any paddock will confirm that the ubiquitous Ford Transit is just about the most practical choice for most club racers. All the various alternatives are just as practical, of course, but there are naturally more secondhand ones about.

A van becomes immediately much more than just the means of shifting the bike to the circuit. A huge number of mates/girlfriends/family can come along and share costs. Indeed, if you can team up with another racer to split all the running costs then the budget immediately assumes much less daunting proportions.

Better though, a van can be turned into a 'paddock hotel' for those overnight meetings with little more than sleeping bags or a mattress. Camping gear stowed in the van occupies little space, while a camping stove can further reduce costs by avoiding snackbar meals. Eating on the road can be something to avoid.

So build into your costs the price of transport, tax, insurance, etc. and don't forget the spare tyres. Petrol for the van and the bike is a not inconsiderable factor. You can quickly reduce the fuel consumption of a big four-stroke to less than 20 mpg when you really give it some stick. And don't forget 'fuel' for the riders too!

A convenient alternative, if you have one, of course, is a car and a trailer. Secondhand trailers can be found in the columns of *Motorcycle News* or *Exchange & Mart* and hooked on to a borrowed or family car will save lots of expense. Drawbacks, though, are that the bike will get really mucky if it pours on the way, and when you are in the paddock, you won't have shelter to work on the bike in the

Mini-stocks allow variety without prohibitive expense. Sponsorship can never start too early or at too low a level

Above **Cost can be contained by being prepared to camp rather than staying in hotels. The camaraderie around the barbeque is one of the delights of racing**

Left **A Ducati like Bill Swallow's can be exhilarating – but pricey**

dry, or have a fry up. Just a thought, check that your insurance covers towing.

Maintaining the bike might not be thought of as an initial expense but is one that cannot be avoided. Certain components in the bike will need to be renewed periodically and should be budgeted for. A two-stroke, for instance, will require pistons and rings every few hundred miles, while a four-stroke with a season or two behind it could need, maybe, a set of con rods. Regard it as insurance, perforated crankcases are more than a mechanical disaster.

3

Sponsorship

This chapter was prompted by many enquiries over the years on how to get sponsorship. What the riders really meant was, 'How do I get someone else to pay for me to enjoy my racing, because I think I'm good'. Indeed, some were even asking the question before they had actually started racing, finding that they couldn't afford a bike but thought that someone else would buy one for them.

So let's start from the beginning. Before you stand a chance of obtaining sponsorship you should ask yourself what advantage the potential sponsor would gain from paying you some of his hard earned cash in order to see his name on your fairing.

You might well be forgiven for thinking that having won, say, lots of club events and perhaps championships, many companies would be pleased to be associated with you simply because you are obviously successful. After all, that's what racing is all about, isn't it? Well the sponsors' answer might well be no!

In the first instance, the companies whose products are used by racers themselves such as oil, petrol and various accessories, should derive some benefit from being associated with their name

World champion Eddie Lawson brilliantly portrays his sponsor's colours. The small 'T' on the rear number plate means that it's his reserve machine

appearing on a successful bike. You will see many familiar stickers on bikes at meetings advertising anything from spark plugs to tyres, to helmets and leathers.

However, the successful clubman can still find it difficult to obtain even basic sponsorship however many races he might win. Think about it, you might have a dynamite machine that blows the opposition into the weeds but if it's covered in oily fingerprints, your leathers are less than immaculate and your general appearance is that of a real scruffbag it won't impress anybody.

That is one aspect, another is that of simply

Below right **British champion Roger Marshall on a Rothmans' Honda. The colours match exactly Rothmans' corporate style. Stickers from more minor sponsors are carried on the bottom of the fairing**

Below **Barry Sheene was not only a world champion, but probably the best rider ever when it came to marketing his own image and that of motorcycle racing in general**

approaching potential sponsors in the right way. You might as well get used to preparing your case for support in the best way possible from the start. Anticipate the time when, as a successful racer, you will be able to go outside the 'trade' to go for the bigger deals that the stars obviously manage to sign up.

The catchword is simply professionalism. You have to prepare your 'presentation' in a professional way. You will have to convince people that may well not know the front end of a bike from the other. In this case you will first have to sell the very idea of motorcycle racing itself before you can even get to first base. You will have to talk in the language that they understand. Remember that your place in their scheme of things will probably be just a small part of their general promotion campaign for their products, whatever they may be. You must be to them promotable material, an image that would do them credit.

As a starter, you will have to build up some sort of dossier. It will contain lots of attractive pictures of you and your machine, not necessarily at some extreme angle of lean, but looking primarily neat and well presented and likely to do credit to anyone

associated with your racing efforts. The pictures will be captioned and supported by a neatly typed supporting commentary on your successes, the club championships you have won and the results achieved, woven into a success story. All this will be contained in a nice glossy scrapbook or photo album.

While Barry Sheene will be thought of as one of yesterday's men to today's racers, he was probably the supreme example of how to market yourself. He managed to get featured on the nation's TV screens more than any other racer and indeed can claim much of the credit for getting the sport on to the television when he was Britain's world champion on two wheels. When he did, he never failed to get his sponsors' names into the act. Sheene was good news for anyone associated with him and consequently he earned the hundreds of thousands of pounds that kept his grand prix racing team on the tracks. Whether he won or lost, he got coverage, and so did his sponsors.

Sheene was something of an exception but one of the best examples that our aspiring racer should bear in mind, even if he was at megastar world championship level. Reading this book suggests

Even hotels in the Isle of Man can act as sponsors by offering accommodation. A credit on the fairing as some repayment and publicity

that you are starting from square one so the search for sponsorship opportunities should start a little nearer home.

For starters, have you considered your employer as a potential sponsor? Laugh! Maybe not. I've even seen bikes decked out in British Gas livery, so even if you work for a corporation all is not lost. Often there are sports and social clubs and I've known these to be a happy hunting ground. One guy I know used to get a substantial sum of money just for putting the name of a well-known lift company on his fairing.

However, it's probably easier if you work for a small company. Once your racing career starts to show some signs of success then your workmates will inevitably have begun to take an interest and the word soon gets round the firm. Since it is a small company, you might even get the chance to show that dossier to the boss himself. If the company is rather bigger then you might try to gain

Left Knight with the *Motorcycle Sport* magazine-sponsored Suzuki GSX-R 1100. Credits to all the accessory suppliers are also visible

Below From the 1987 San Marino GP, French ace Raymond Roche shows just how you can use a company logo on a bike to good effect

the interest of, say, the departmental manager or personnel manager. You could start by suggesting that maybe some of the staff would like to come down to the local track to see the action. The bike, of course, will be immaculate and dressed up in the company livery – for a couple of hundred pounds to cover the costs of getting the bike professionally painted, that is.

Since you are now racing, you will inevitably end up buying lots of spares and bits and pieces from your nearest friendly local dealer – if he isn't, change him. You'll soon get to know the staff behind the counter and that's the way in. Don't be surprised, though, if it takes a little time, they've probably heard it all before. Now this is where your dossier, produced at the right time, will get you in ahead of the others. This proves that you really do race and maybe gets you to see the boss. Now you can go with your hard selling tactics with the obvious benefits of having the name of the business and telephone number written large on your fairing.

Simply try to generate further interest, or business, among the thousands of potential customers who will see the bike racing. It is also sometimes a useful ploy to suggest that the bike would create extra interest and business if the bike was displayed in the showroom, when it wasn't actually

being used. Now you will really see why the bike must be kept in pristine condition.

By now you may well be talking of having your bike specially painted in the colours of your sponsor and to complete the picture your leathers should also be part of the general 'scheme'. Before you suggest this, they should be paid for by the sponsor and in addition to anything you might get in the way of hard cash to help you run the bike.

So the lesson is, learn to sell yourself and motorcycling in general. Put yourself in the position of a potential sponsor. Find reasons why they should want to put money into your racing efforts. After all, that's where we came in, why should *they* pay for *you* to race – you have to convince them that it would be of benefit to *them*.

4

What to race

Just about the most popular way to get into racing these days is in the production classes, and the 250 cc class in particular. This has a lot going for it simply because 250 road bikes such as the Yamaha and Suzuki are cheap to buy and run. In any case it is a bike that riders will have had experience of when road riding and indeed, may still own. Above all it offers the sort of performance most will feel comfortable with while starting to learn the craft of road racing.

New models are launched so frequently these days that to recommend a particular road bike as the best one to start with would probably mean that these words of wisdom become out of date in

Sidecar racing can provide the means for two to play at the same time – and to share the expense. The fun can be just as fast and furious

Motorcycle sport is open to both men and women. Laura Brightman shows just how to push an LC Yamaha in 250 cc production racing. Probably one of the cheapest options

The Honda CB600 series is an inexpensive way of getting machinery into national championship competition. Only minor changes are allowed for this class

a very short time. But the principle will hold good, buy what is the popular road bike – and what is more, what is currently winning the class.

One reservation here is that while the Honda Dream was for many years the best-selling 250 roadster, as a racer it would have stood no chance at all among the other production bikes. A better example would have been the Yamaha LCs that the majority of racers cut their racing teeth on at one time. Plenty of performance, they could be made to go much faster with little cost and were relatively inexpensive to run. Now the YZR model is superseding the LC and the RGV is replacing the also very popular Suzuki Gamma.

In an ideal world production racing would be between unmodified bikes, with the performance exactly as it was on leaving the manufacturer. However, the fact is that the two-strokes have been the happy hunting ground for the many tuners who advertise in magazines specializing in production racing. Unfortunately for the purists, the result has been a considerable increase in performance to the point where anyone racing a 'bog standard' model would stand little chance of keeping up. The only

thing that can be said in favour of such tuning is that it does not cost too much.

Let me say straightaway that unless you are something of a lawyer and try to read things into the current ACU Production Machine regulations that are not there, tuning is really not permitted. However, since it would be virtually impossible to check the insides of a motor in the paddock at a race meeting, and in any case the volunteers who check machine specifications might well not know the difference anyway, tuning does, in fact, take place. This is mainly in the smaller classes where the two-strokes respond much more readily, in the big classes it is more difficult and in any case it's much more down to the rider's ability to use the considerable performance already available.

The classes in production racing do vary a little from club to club. Some have a capacity class 'cut' from over 250 to 600, over 600 to 750 and over 750 to 1300 cc. Some clubs are able to run races for just 250 cc production bikes, they are so popular. Others lump them all together, it usually depends on the amount of entries they get in each class as to whether a grid can be filled. Scan the programmes

Single-cyclinder racing machines are catered for in many clubs and offer the chance to build up a bike from a scrap roadster. This Hossack special frame will house a variety of motors and has won many times in the hands of Vernon Glashier

Classic racing is growing in popularity. Here Tony Price hustles a BSA twin. Competition embraces club, national and international races for classic machines as well as the Classic Manx Grand Prix

to spot how your chosen club organizes things, they might not suit your plans, or current machine.

For instance, it is all very gratifying to win your class, but if it happens to be in about 15th overall position, because on a 250 you are up against all the bigger bikes, then it's hardly as gratifying as actually being the first past the chequered flag. The other side of the coin to this is also the fact that if you do actually finish first, the chances are that you will at least be mentioned in the press results on the meeting which will enable you to start a cuttings file of your successes. So although you may well beat the others, it won't do your prospects half as good as really winning. And that might be down to choosing the right club and circuit. A little home-work really can make all the difference to your prospects.

Once you start to move up to the bigger four-stroke classes things start to change radically. This is mainly because the performance increase is appreciable, but so is the size of the bike. It's all very well to scratch like mad on the limit on a 250 production bike but when the bike consists of around 400 lb of metal and has a 150 mph potential

there are far fewer riders who can really handle that sort of performance.

This means that while the dicing within the field is not quite so close, the guys up front who can really handle a 750 will be dicing nose to tail at somewhat elevated speeds compared to the previous 250s. The extra performance starts to sort out the men from the boys, as they say. However, it has to be said that the latest 750s handle so well once you're used to them that they can almost be ridden like a 250, that is, if you really have what it takes.

When you move into the 1300 cc class, you will have as much power as the riders who really go for it up front in any national event in the country. In fact when you consider that in 1988 Geoff Johnson put in a 116 mph lap in the Isle of Man on a production Yamaha, it is little short of mind-blowing because that sort of performance is only just short of the level of top riders on top machinery in the open racing class. If you really can use one of these 130 bhp 160 mph monsters then you certainly have talent.

From the straightforward production classes

there are several 'stock' classes derived directly from it, though it has to be said that these can firstly be expensive, and secondly extremely competitive right up to international level. In fact, hardly the way to start your racing career.

However, there are various Formula classes and Superstocks. Both were started with the idea that production based classes would reduce the escalating costs of racing, particularly at grand prix and international level. TT Formulas 1, 2 and 3 were originally world championship classes based on capacity classes; F3 soon faded out, F2 lasted a couple of years longer and all three were inspired by the Isle of Man's need to maintain a world championship event. While F1 has become a credible racing class, for 1989 it was scheduled to be included in the new Superbike Championship series, the first race of which was staged at Donington at Easter 1988.

Superbikes and Superstocks are similar in many ways; both use the standard cycle. The former allow heavy frame modifications, the latter less so but it can't be too long before they merge. The Superstock class originally allowed little tuning, but this seems to have become gradually relaxed and the strip-it-and-tune-the-motor approach is likely to be the way into more prestigious classes. However, the mere fact of competing at a higher level will inevitably mean spending much more cash to 'keep up with the Joneses'.

Nevertheless, you can still find clubs that do run races for the various Formula class machines: 1, 2 and 3. In any case, the grids are largely filled with production bikes and F2 and F3 are largely dead now; they used to be for up to 600 cc four-strokes, 350 cc two-strokes, 400 cc four-strokes and 250 cc two-strokes.

Now the 'open' classes are simply restrictions on capacity only, you can, as the name implies, do anything at all to cycle and motor. And if you happen to have almost any machine available that you want to play with, doing just anything you fancy to it, then this can be a good idea for a racing start.

The racing classes are, as mentioned, governed

The LC Yamaha has provided the way into racing for many racers and nowadays there are events for stripped-down versions. These provide an inexpensive way to start

only by the current regulations that restrict fuel to petrol and the current safety requirements as listed in road racing regulations, and capacity. These are up to 125 cc, though the 80 cc class does occasionally feature, up to 250 cc, to 350 cc and then unlimited, which is up to 1300 cc. At national or international level, the top capacity may well be 500 cc, like the grand prix classes.

You can have a lot of fun with any bike, throwing off all the road bits and tuning the engine just to see how fast you can make the thing go, but if the intention is winning, then the choice is limited, even at club level.

This is mainly because in the 250 cc and 350 cc classes, the bike that wins is likely to be, for some considerable time, the racing versions of the LC Yamaha, designated 'TZ'. They win the smaller classes and tuned big road bikes or production bikes, or 'roadie' engines in racing chassis, win the 1300 cc class.

Above **While classic racing can be a cheap way to start, to win at top level you need a Matchless G50 costing thousands of pounds. Dave Roper stars here**

Above right **Racing a BSA Bantam may be cheapest of all. The Bantam Racing Club provides a full season of racing. Mike Poxon shows how it's done at Snetterton**

Right **Knight has tried the joys of 'chair' racing, seen here hanging out of the side of a Vincent-powered outfit – with broken zip on his leathers**

Single-cylinder racing

That is certainly not the extent of the choice from which to make your racing debut. Many clubs will feature a race for single-cylinder machines and these can certainly provide an inexpensive yet fiercely competitive class of racing which means lots of fun. These are the various big four-stroke and two-stroke engines that appear in every manufacturer's range. They are tuned as far as they will go and with the chassis modified (sometimes a racing chassis is used) the racing is fast and furious, competitive and above all, fun. And since there is only one of everything to replace, it's comparatively cheap.

Bantams

Bantam racing is yet another alternative. As the name implies, it is derived from the old BSA Bantam machines, the 125 two-strokes. There is a club devoted to this form of racing and it really is less expensive than most others. Funnily enough, it is called the Bantam Racing Club. If the idea of 100 mph maximum speeds appeals in a fairly close knit club, then it would be a good idea to join and buy one of the retiring members' bikes since there aren't too many about. They are always available at the end of every season, advertised in the club magazine columns.

Sidecars

Sidecar racing is a highly specialized class. The technology is more akin to three-wheeled racing cars but unlike solos it's a team game and it certainly has its appeal. Not all clubs run a class for them though, there aren't always enough bodies in a club racing 'chairs' to fill a grid so the club can't afford to put on a race where there is poor attendance: each grid has to be reasonably full to pay its way and justify its inclusion in the programme.

At club level almost any size and sort of motor finds its way into the chassis and a big four-stroke can be a cheap way in and quite competitive. The *most* competitive though will be the bigger two-strokes, usually Yamaha, of 500cc and the older 750s, which just seem to go on and on.

Classic motorcycles are not only European as this Yamaha shows

A fairly recent alternative is so-called F2 Sidecar racing in which twin-cylinder 350 cc two-stroke and 1000 cc four-stroke engines are used. The simple twin-cylinder motor is cheap to run and yet it succeeds in pushing two bodies and the chassis around quite quickly. There's even a class for them in some international meetings, principally the Isle of Man TT where they run along with all the others, but there is a class within the entry for them.

High-speed trials

It's true we are talking about getting into racing, and while speed trials are not strictly speaking races, there is an awful lot of dicing that goes on. It's using your road bike, it's cheap, fun, not too fiercely competitive and it's the way in for many who can't afford to do anything else. At least until the bug really bites and a serious debut is the only way forward to satisfy your ego.

There are several clubs who run speed trials, and indeed it's the way I first got the taste myself, back

in 1958. Clubs like the Vincent Owners and the Motor Cycling Club, Velocette and Triumph Owners all put on days for their members to enjoy themselves racing against the clock to achieve set speed schedules for trophies.

Classic or vintage racing

You can race anything, and why not an old British bike? There are in fact lots of races for them. Even a national championship and bikes at that level, under the stimulus of modern technology and materials they are going faster than ever. You can even race in the Isle of Man in the Classic Manx Grand Prix. Now the recently launched International Historic Racing Organisation is getting races staged at grands prix. Classic bikes are undergoing something of a revival.

While I do occasionally race a Triumph Daytona in these events, it is something of a specialist field and if it's your interest, I would advise you to join an appropriate club to acquaint yourself with all the classes and specifications.

Certainly it can be one of the less expensive ways to go racing, but you would be kidding yourself if you thought the guys at the top didn't spend thousands on their sport and went all out to win. In the midfield, it is more fun than in most classes. The atmosphere really is quite different, and worth experiencing.

Classic Matchless G50 in all its naked glory. You can actually buy a 'new' remanufactured model. Replacement parts to original specifications are now made to keep them racing. But it is certainly not a cheap way to go racing

5

Preparation

While the maximum power from your standard motor is necessary to put you at least on par with the opposition, the plan should be first just to compete, that is to complete the races and gain the necessary experience to progress. A visit to any club paddock will reveal many riders seemingly working on their bikes all day, whether they never touch the bike all week and intend to do all their maintenance in the paddock on the day, I've never quite discovered. Of course it's always possible that they are the odd one per cent of riders who are not expert mechanics.

We all like to think that we know how the bike ticks but like riding ability, mechanical ability is not evenly spread around the paddock. Deciding your own level of incompetence requires an honesty with yourself that may save you hundreds of pounds and more than a few race retirements.

So if you believe you are up to stripping and rebuilding a water-cooled, four-cylinder, double ohc 16-valve motor and can get the valve timing spot on, great, many can't. If your bike is a new one, then of course you can expect the motor to be good for at least a season with no more than basic maintenance like frequent oil changes and checking of valve clearances.

Our race preparation, then, will primarily be devoted to the cycle but there's plenty involved to keep you busy and to make the difference in competitiveness.

This shows how it certainly should not be done; in the paddock. Do not put tools down on to the ground where they pick up grit and dirt that can find its way into the engine

Whether you are racing a production or open class bike, you can choose to run standard road, or even racing tyres, and you can see a mixture around the paddocks. Tyres can make a real difference to the handling of your bike. The wrong profile or section can transform a bike from a pussycat to an ill-handling beast and vice versa. Certainly the wrong choice of tyres for the day can make the difference between coming home first, or coming nowhere.

That choice may not be quite as simple as it seems even if you do decide to stick with road tyres. The choice between Metzeler, Michelin, Pirelli, Avon or Dunlop can be difficult and quite subjective. Seeing what the opposition fits is the best guide in the short term until you have enough experience to make up your own mind as to what suits your riding style – and that, too, can make a difference.

Again, it's still not quite as simple as that. Even when using road tyres, there are still likely to be choices apart from the make. Some manufacturers offer a choice of 'sport' compounds, and that simply means softer rubber that will give more grip. The trouble with that though is that they wear out more quickly.

At club level though there is one extra choice, and that is the fitting of 'wet' tyres. These are of a much softer compound and patterned very heavily to enable water to be dispersed and reduce the risk of aquaplaning. They make an incredible difference, so much so that even club riders find the need to carry a spare set of wheels fitted with wets and it's just this sort of situation where if it rains and the others have wets and you haven't, you may as well watch the race.

Riders will quickly find the need to learn all the mysterious numbers imprinted on the walls of tyres made especially for racing because they denote the various compounds: soft, intermediate, hard and several in-between. However, it is worth asking yourself whether the extra expense of racing tyres is justified because those produced for today's big roadsters really are good enough to test the limits of many riders' abilities.

At club level the choice is limited to tyres with tread patterns, and riders are deemed to be insufficiently experienced to use any more grip until having acquired a national status licence, when competing at races at this level, slick or non-patterned tyres are allowed. Slick tyres do offer more grip, but even these come in various grades of

Engine tuning as it is done by an expert with all the necessary facilities. Shown is an engine mounted on a dynamometer used for testing power output

Tyres

For the raw beginner with a road bike, even the manufacturer's original equipment should be good enough, at least, to find out what it's all about before spending a lot of money searching for the make that gives the ultimate grip. Most club events allow a free choice of tyres but there are series in which there are stipulations that only allow the use of tyres from a manufacturer who is the sponsor of that particular series.

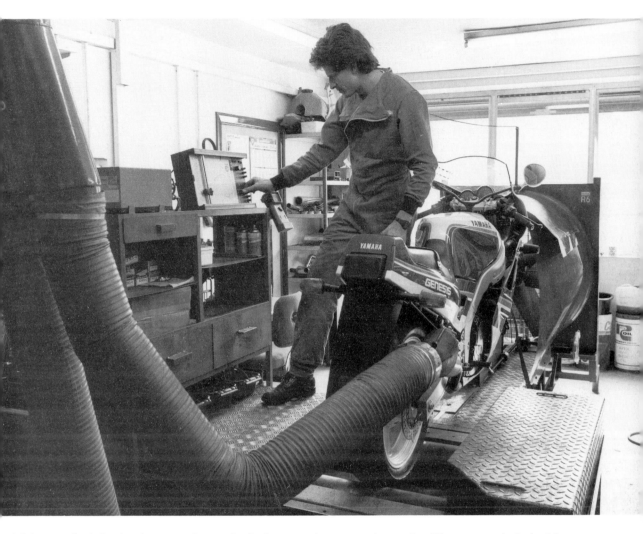

This Yamaha is having its state of tune checked on a Motod dynamometer. The mechanic is using sophisticated electronic diagnosis equipment that checks engine settings

rubber mix. On a hot day, a hard mix would be required, getting softer as the temperature lowers.

The reasons why are pretty straightforward. Tyres work better at particular 'working' temperatures. The heat is generated within the tyre by the movement of the naturally flexible material and the greater the movement, the higher the temperature attained. When a tyre overheats the grip will be greatly reduced because the overheating effectively over 'cures' the rubber changing its grip-

ping properties, to simplify a most technical subject.

A tyre with treads will allow the rubber to move about more, and more heat will therefore be generated and to apply that to our wet tyres, if conditions change and it dries out while the race is on, a wet tyre will rapidly overheat as the soft rubber and deep treads generate too much heat and they may well start to disintegrate within a few laps.

It is worth noting, that even some road tyres used for racing, once having reached the point of getting very hot, (enough that is to start sliding earlier than usual), will never be quite as good again and are effectively useless. Certainly top racers will only use a set of tyres once, though this primarily means professional men in open events. The rest of us could probably not afford to spend £100 or so per tyre per race, and no doubt even that figure will soon be out of date.

One last thought on tyres, an unbalanced wheel can upset a bike and if you fit them yourself don't forget this vital operation. It means removing the wheel and balancing it, mounted on the spindle, so that it is free to rotate quite freely. There are rigs specially for this with bearings upon which the spindle rests, to eliminate the friction of the bearing seals.

It may be that leaving the wheel in the forks and making sure the pads are not in contact with the wheel will leave it sufficiently free to try it yourself. Spin the wheel slowly and it will settle with the heaviest part of the wheel at the bottom, naturally. The objective is to stick lead weights on the opposite side, to even out the imbalance of tyre, valve and rim.

Brakes

Principal subjects here are pads, discs, hydraulics and brake lines, unless of course you choose classic racing when it'll be drums, cables and linings, which are quite a subject in themselves.

Just like the various grades of rubber in tyres, there are various grades of material in the brake pads available. Again there are similarities in that some will grip better than others but wear out faster.

Where tyres overheat and lose their grip, so do pads, but what they do is to 'glaze up'. There is no mistaking the situation; braking deteriorates rapidly as to be comparatively non-existent and when the pads are examined the surface will appear as though it's been polished.

There's really no alternative but to replace them, though if stuck at a meeting with no spares, filing off the glaze will partially retrieve things for a while.

Rather like tyres, the original equipment fitted really is quite good enough for road use and while on a 'learning curve' in road racing.

Discs

Production racers are stuck with what they have, open class men seeking the last bit of performance may want to go for the lightest they can find with two objectives in view: to improve performance through achieving a better power to weight ratio and to improve roadholding by reducing unsprung

weight. If the latter requires a little explanation, it's simply that the suspension system will perform better if it has less weight to control. The forks bounce up and down rapidly travelling over a rough track or road and that movement has to be controlled or it would upset the roadholding. With less work to do the suspension will be more effective.

The options here are to have a pattern of holes drilled in discs that are solid (don't try it unless you have a professional standard workshop) which will effectively take a fair bit of weight off. Patterns of 60 holes are offered by the various racing services available from small engineering companies.

More expensive options are those of obtaining discs made from lighter materials, frequently aluminium with a harder metal coating. Another option under development is carbon fibre and while such expensive and comparatively exotic materials are usually the province of the works teams, carbon fibre fairings are no longer unusual and do offer quite substantial weight savings.

Discs are now just about as thin as they might realistically be, bearing in mind the stresses they have to withstand and the temperatures to which they are constantly subjected. The frequent heating and cooling nevertheless sometimes leads to a warping of the discs. This can require frequent pumping of the brake lever approaching a corner as the pads have been pushed back from contact with the discs by, in effect, their sideways oscillations.

It only requires a few 'thou' runout for this situation to arise and if it's only this small amount it's

Left Tuning a two-stroke is something of a 'black art' and this picture shows the difference between a standard and tuned barrel

Right It is permissible to fit hydraulic steering dampers on production racing machines, allowed on the grounds of safety

Below Brakes must be in absolutely optimum condition before you race

possible to have them skimmed to get them running true again. That small engineering company again is the only answer short of scrapping them.

The vital link in the system is the fluid and the hoses through which it is conveyed. Even in a production machine it is possible to change the brake hoses for braided lines to reduce wall flexing which can be quite a factor in the sponginess frequently found in standard machines. Goodridge are well known for their hoses and racing services.

Brake fluid can be a vital factor and there are various grades over and above that usually recommended as standard in manufacturer's maintenance manuals. At the least it's worth changing whatever is already in the system for one of the

Special frames are made by companies like Spondon as an improvement in handling and weight-saving. They can be made to accommodate almost any motor

racing grades which will resist better the much higher temperatures generated by racing competition. Standards are denoted by 'dot grades' and a number and the many companies in the business of marketing competition oils, like Shell, Castrol and Bel-Ray offer competition grades.

It is also worth noting that brake fluid absorbs water, is hygroscopic, and after a time, certainly once a season, it should be changed. By remedying a combination of small deficiencies such as 'weak' hoses, tired fluid and perhaps just a minute quantity of air or water in the system and a trace of runout on a disc, it can transform a brake from being spongy and just about adequate to one that will stop you on the proverbial sixpence.

It is often easier to eliminate sponginess from a mechanical system, than from a modern hydraulic system. Classic racing has become quite a specialized art spurred on somewhat by the accessibility of new materials that were not available at the time the bikes were manufactured and some of the performances now possible are improvements on the original components.

Brakes are certainly one area where later compounds are an improvement on the original. For maximum braking linings should be fitted by a racing competition service where long-established people like Ferodo will fit new material to your shoes and then machine the surface for 100 per cent contact with the drum.

Cables and linkages speak for themselves in reducing flexing but spotting what the successful competition is using really is the way to find out what's best.

Suspension

Production machine competitors only have grades of oil and springs to worry about but even just the grade of oil in the front forks can make a significant difference to the bike's roadholding. We'll make the assumption that the quantity of oil will be as specified in the handbook and that accurate quantities will be in either fork leg, because things as basic as that frequently get overlooked.

Bearing in mind that the grade of oil 'fitted' as standard by the manufacturers is best suited to road use and may have been chosen to cope with two up riding or even the great disparities between rider weights, it can frequently be changed with advantage. Most popular will be one that is a grade or two thicker and of a competition variety, since this will be designed to cut down frothing or airation as the oil is forced through small apertures in the valves within the forks to control the front wheel hopping up and down.

Anti-dive and pre-load settings abound on some machines and something as simple as winding up the fork spring pre-load setting can make both a difference to roadholding and indeed ground clearance. Some handbooks will give recommendations for hard riding etc., these will be worth taking note of but don't always assume that the maximum or hardest setting is necessarily the best. As it happens, my Suzuki GSX-R 1100 responds best on a hard setting.

Alternative springs, too, are another factor and some riders use them, some with dual ratings, achieved by the coils being wound closer together towards the ends of the coils. The aim being to give a spring that works over a wider poundage range than a one-range rated spring, say 80 lb as against an 80–100 lb. Adding packing to springs to pre-load them is another small dodge in fine tuning roadholding.

It can be a mistake to get involved in such mysteries before you get well into the business and find out what you are about. Most production machines merely require fine tuning to get better results, rather than modifications which may be questioned. The essence of setting up bikes is usually to control the suspension's movement by heavier damping settings rather than heavy springs because the heavier they are, the harder it will be for the damping system to control the movement. Control is the essence.

Rear springing was made simpler with the introduction of monoshock designs since making sure both units were exactly the same was always a concern. However, it has introduced a complication that many riders run into. Units on the big bikes usually have the spring pre-load adjusted by threaded rings which screw up to compress the spring, something that seems to be tried by many and the source of many a mis-handling machine.

Current club production regulations actually allow the changing of suspension units and there are several on the market like White Power and Ohlins which, for a reasonable amount, do offer improvements. In the case of the GSX-R 750 Suzuki, the standard unit would fade under the heat of hard competition and these racing units are designed to prevent that. In the case of the 1100 model, the remote reservoir prevents overheating.

Bearings

There is one particular set of bearings that certainly will affect any bike's performance – the head races. Even if you've done thousands of road miles and never found the need, when racing it's worth

keeping a regular check on these items. The smallest shake will be magnified and roadholding will quickly deteriorate.

Wheel bearings also require checking before taking to the tarmac and if renewing them, or just checking and cleaning, use a high melting-point grease just in case the heat generated by extra heavy braking leads to it melting and finding its way past the seals and on to the brake material.

Finally, the swinging-arm pivot. These bearings are as vital as the head bearings and a potential source of bad roadholding. Combine a small amount of detectable shake in all of them and no wonder your model wobbles and others don't. This may be obvious but what is acceptable, or undetectable on the road, just won't do if you intend trying to keep up with the front runners.

Steering dampers

These are seen by many as the panacea for disguising the deficiencies of a bike that wobbles or weaves. What it's doing is certainly not curing the problem, but reducing it to manageable proportions. Having said that, the experts will ride a bike so hard that while they already have the best handling set-up that their machine is capable of, they manage to drive so close to disaster that anything will weave and wobble over a rough surface, like the Isle of Man. Fitting a damper can in those circumstances make the difference of several miles per hour through a corner.

It is possible to fit a damper even on to a production class machine, permitted on the grounds of safety. You can actually buy kits to fit most machines but having owned many a really fast production bike I am not convinced of their necessity except for the Isle of Man which is so much of an exception in racing terms that there's a special chapter on it (see p. 74).

Above left This is a racing rarity in 1988, a rotary-engined Norton. Campaigned so far only by the works, production models will be available for those who want to buy something different. The engine is basically that used in police patrol bikes

Left A fluorescent strip of tape on the tachometer can be a useful reminder about the location of the powerband. Or as a warning not to over-rev

General preparation

Without doubt the motor will be pushed to its limit so extra care for it is essential; engine failure is not just potentially very expensive but it could also lead to an accident should it happen in the heat of close competition. An investment in regular changes of oil and filters is simply insurance against having to spend much more on engine repairs, not to mention missed races and wasted entry fees.

Every component in the motor or on the cycle has a limited working life and therefore needs to be maintained accordingly, which means that every one of them will have to be replaced eventually. If you are running a racing/open class machine it is very worthwhile trying to ascertain just how many miles it has done before you buy it. The major engine components like connecting rods, pistons and engine bearings certainly won't last forever and the consequences of failure don't bear thinking about but at every meeting somebody dumps oil on the track, and that usually means that whatever contained the oil is now in a state of disrepair – frequently the crankcase. Think about it!

Production racers can reckon on their new machines giving them, perhaps, a couple of busy seasons before having to replace connecting rods and other major components. If they are two-strokes then life is far more limited, particularly if the local hotshot tuner has got his hands on it. A really highly strung model may well require almost as frequent treatment as models such as the Yamaha 'TZ' pukka racing models, not to mention four-cylinder Suzuki racing replicas.

'Zeds' and the aforementioned replica grand prix racers have a very limited number of racing hours allocated to each component. To keep a highly strung Zed in top fettle might mean changing the piston rings every 150 miles, pistons every 300 miles and rods and crankshafts at least every time four figure racing miles are covered. It's true that many will last longer, but then the edge will certainly be taken off. Performances vary a great deal depending on the amount of time and cash spent on a racing stroker; my 1100 will pass 75 per cent of 350 Yamaha TZs at a club meeting but when put up against a really sharp model at a national meeting there's little to choose between them.

Chains

These are always a potential source of trouble though the sealed link endless variety fitted to big 'roadies' have solved many of the problems of yesteryear. In fact, I find that a new one will sometimes go for two seasons before stretch dictates renewal.

Open racers often fall into the trap of running spring links because they will frequently change sprockets for different circuits. Actually, the trap lies not in their usage but in the regularity with which they are replaced. Even riveted soft links let go at unexpected moments and have to be checked every few meetings. The spray-on lubricant marketed by, say, Shell is good insurance and may even reduce friction a little and save the odd half brake horsepower, to say nothing of a reduction in sprocket wear.

Fairings

These are vital on racing machines to give you something on which to paint your name and your sponsors' names. On a production bike they can save hundreds of pounds worth of damage to the rest of the bike should you exceed your own expertise. More to the point, though, they actually make the bike a little faster on a fast circuit.

However, fairings like all the bolted-on components are a potential source of trouble, which is to say that they are only trouble when they come off. Frequently removed components means that frequently used nuts and bolts are liable to come unwound, and could do so in the middle of a race. Do replace them as a little, inexpensive, insurance at regular intervals.

General

Other nuts and bolts will be unwound and replaced frequently. It may be that you remove brake calipers regularly to take off the front wheel, and one of those bolts coming undone in a race could prove to be lethal. As a precaution, you will notice that many machines have these vital nuts and bolts drilled and wired up to make quite sure that they don't come undone when you don't want them to.

One bolt that certainly *will* be drilled and wired in position is the sump oil drain plug. This is mandatory and you won't get past the scrutineer unless you do it. It's the one thing he really will check.

A sturdy, well-constructed stand is indispensible. There is no point in saving a few pounds on one which is not man enough for the job. It will only let you down at a critical point

6

What to wear

Protective clothing – leathers, helmet, gloves and boots, is in many ways more important than the bike. You can mend a bike when you bend it, but mending bodies is always more painful and not necessarily always 100 per cent successful. To see the state of some of the riders' gear around the paddock, though, you can only assume that they are in happy ignorance of the potential consequences that their inadequate clothing could incur, and scruffy leathers certainly won't lure a possible sponsor.

Helmets

There's an old saying, 'if you have a ten pound head buy a ten pound helmet', which shows you how old it really is. But the message is a gem. Nevertheless, price is not the only arbiter and buying an expensive 'lid' from the States does not always guarantee you are getting something of a superior quality to any other. Mind you, you might be forgiven for thinking that helmet A is better than helmet B, simply because the current world champion wears one. However, if he had a lucrative contract with a helmet manufacturer it would certainly have an influence on his choice.

There is one particular factor that you will have to take into account, although it won't really affect your choice of a good helmet. It's simply that it must reach the current safety standards required by the ACU and to denote those that have reached certain required British Standards, it will bear the ACU Gold Stamp of approval. When your helmet is checked at a meeting, the scrutineer will look for this, among other things.

The other things? Well, for a start, does it really fit securely? This might sound like an obvious question and I'm sure that yours is comfortable, but that's not the same thing by any means. Some of the more searching scrutineers will ask you to wear your helmet and try and pull it off your head. They will try to rotate it forward over your head, because if it doesn't fit snugly it could come off in a spill. It's just like rotating a bucket over its handle as the helmet pivots over the strap.

The scrutineer will also check the general condition of your lid for signs that it has been 'tested' sliding down the road. Bumps and scratches are bad news. A helmet is designed to absorb blows and does so in the extreme by progressively collapsing. It might only be bruised now by what seemed to be a minor bump previously, but its your neck and maybe it won't do the same job twice. If the scrutineer does object, well it's your safety he's concerned with, so don't complain because you have to buy a new one, it's for your own good.

Choosing one with the latest in ventilation may be a good idea as misting up can certainly be a problem in some circumstances. It affects some people more than others, spectacle wearers more than most as I can testify. Under heavy rain conditions it can cost you a race and has done so for many of the star riders. At the time of writing no helmet is completely free of the possibility of misting up.

There are many suggested remedies to prevent misting. As mentioned, some of the latest helmets have vents at the front that duct fresh air up the inside and are supposed to keep the visor clear. But even the best have been known to fail under the worst conditions. My own remedy is one you'll see around the paddocks and seldom fails. It is simply to stick a piece of 'duct tape' over your nose and on to the helmet to form a barrier to the hot breath that will condense on the visor if it reaches it. Duct tape? This is silver tape usually used by heating and ventilation engineers to seal the joints between sections of piping, or ducts.

Some manufacturers have models with a built-in, or even removable, section that is supposed to close the gap in the same way as the tape. However, they do rely on a perfect fit to the face to be effective, you may have the right shape of face, if not you'll have to resort to sticky tape.

Another facet of helmet design concerns the visor which, naturally, you flip up when not on the move. It is worth really checking out whatever ratchet design it might incorporate to ensure that it is really effective and doesn't flop down when you don't want it to. Mine is just tight enough to leave open on the last position when I'm on the grid, so there's no chance of misting, and as soon as a good speed is reached it will close automatically under wind pressure.

One more tip on cleaning visor, specs and helmet paintwork. I use a household wax furniture spray which even has some anti-misting effect too.

Where the future in helmet design is concerned

Above Trevor Nation shows how knee-sliders can actually be used as an extra support when racing on the very limit

Right 1988 world champion Wayne Gardner shows some of the best and most expensive leathers you can buy; Kushitani, from Hammamatsu in Japan. At the time they could cost over £1000

the new technology lies in materials and who knows what else. But there is one factor that will always be worth taking into account, simply the weight. Helmets weigh several pounds and that weight on the end of your spine could easily compound an injury to the neck if the stress inflicted while sliding down the road is of the 'whiplash' variety. The heavier the helmet the greater the potential injury. Obviously, the lighter it can be while still affording adequate impact protection the better.

Leathers

While many substitutes have been tried, leather is the best material to protect your skin from abrasions if you do come unstuck. Many a time you will have seen some poor rider slide down the road at high velocity, roll over and pick himself up apparently no worse for wear. Frequently the only signs of injury are scuffs down the leather racing suit.

Many of the remarks applying to helmets also apply to leathers; in short you can't buy quality cheaply and in any case economizing here is economizing on safety. And I'm afraid if you do intend racing seriously, well someday you'll taste the tarmac. When you do, you'll be thankful for every millimetre of leather (and other things which I'll talk about later in the chapter) between you and the road, believe me.

Almost without exception the leather will be cowhide. Goat and horse are occasionally used but cow seems to be most popular for the course. Don't buy cheap sheepskin, it'll barely survive one moderate spill and it does tear comparatively easily.

Leather racing suits have extra padding fitted where you're most likely to need it; elbows, knees and hips. Ideally, it should be just leather reinforcement but you do get packing in between the layers that may make the suit seem as though it's really thick, but all you get in between the layers is padding that contributes little to saving your skin or even adding to impact resistance.

How can you tell a good suit? By close inspection, checking that the hide is of a consistent thickness throughout, and the thicker the better. Check the stitching: is it even? Make sure it doesn't stray too near the edge of the section of leather. Is it lined, and is the lining cotton? Substitutes such as nylon can be a problem where severe abrasion occurs as the heat generated melts it on a wound. It pays to buy quality.

The most recent trend in racing protection involves adding various formulations of plastic to the vital spots. For instance, you will see the knees in suits fitted with pockets into which plastic cups can be inserted, to protect the vulnerable kneecaps from impact damage. You might like to specify then that your suit has room inside the elbows so that sections of plastic can be inserted to fit snugly around them, thus giving added protection to an area which frequently collects bruises or worse.

Finally, there are various bits of plastic that you

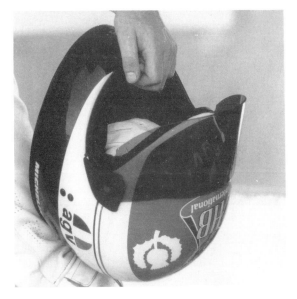

can wear inside your suit for added protection and I strongly recommend a back protector. This is shaped to add padding around the kidneys and the length of the spine and incorporates some sort of belt. Some are purely one thickness of plastic while more recent ones incorporate a much tougher strip down the spine that really does offer mechanical protection. At the time of writing I only knew of one of this kind which is called Moprof. There are also sections available to cover the chest.

One item that straps on to the outside of the leg, which you may have seen, is commonly referred to as a knee-slider and it usually made of nylon or similar and when strapped to the outside of the lower leg allows top professionals to actually slide the bike a fraction by taking a little of the weight on the pad while cornering. Again, more of the esoterics of that later.

Gloves

Glove quality is paramount, and this time it really can make a most painful difference because somehow your hands always seem to take a beating. Even a minor spill can have you sliding on your hands as you try to get up and out of the way of following traffic. Thin ones are attractive, especially during the summer, but don't be tempted. Neither would you want too thick a pair that makes throttle control clumsy.

Quality gloves have extra sections of material over the vital bits such as palms and knuckles and some even have brass 'buttons' fitted where your hand might be expected to impact on the road as extra protection. This could be a good idea but ensure that there's plenty of leather underneath, or any friction would generate heat and burns.

Do make sure that the gloves are not too short, so that there is no gap between your sleeves and glove and if that isn't obvious envisage the situation sliding down the track where one or other rides up. You do need reasonable overlap.

Boots

Not too many points to remember except that your road riding boots may well not be suitable as nothing metal is allowed in the soles, to prevent potential sparks igniting spilt fuel. Also, while many boots do have rubber soles some don't and as long as some races are started by 'run and bump', leather can be very slippery. Fit rubber.

Top AGV helmets are worn by some of the best, including the HB International-sponsored grand prix team – note the logo!

Above Almost any design is possible in leather to please a sponsor – even a Viking

Left Niall McKenzie demonstrates how super you can look when you are part of the Honda works team. Note the perforations that allow him to keep cool in hot weather. Not too good in cold weather!

7

Paperwork, entries and insurance

Our aspiring hero has obtained a licence and gone through all the necessary formalities to get it, but still lacks a vital ingredient, an actual entry for a race – that place on the grid.

In some branches of motorcycle sport you can turn up on the day, cough up the entry fee, sign the form and ride; road racing is not like that. In Chapter 8, the procedure is explained on how you first have to get your competition licence and to do that you have to go through the formalities of joining a club.

Having now become a club member you will probably automatically receive the necessary entry forms, though it's not always the case and you may still have to apply to the club secretary for them. Some clubs will send them all out in booklet form at the beginning of the season and all you have to do is to keep a close check on the dates, when entries should be completed by and sent in, and make sure you do.

That is not the end of the story though. The mere fact of having correctly filled in your form and sent it off in good time doesn't guarantee you that spot on the grid. It's more than likely that others will want to race in your event, otherwise you won't have anyone to beat. So that may mean that it's the luck of the draw as to whether it was your entry form that came out of the pile first.

After the closing date for entries, which will be stated somewhere on your regulations, perhaps a week later, you should hear whether you've been lucky. You might hear, for instance, that you have been placed on the reserve list. That may mean that you still have a reasonable chance of a ride because the organizers will have an educated idea of how many reserves do take places vacated by non-starters. These are usually the mechanical failures that take their toll on the day, or the unfortunate riders who ended up on the tarmac, without their bikes.

However, being a reserve does mean that you have the option of withdrawing from the race if you so choose. This could be worthwhile if the race was the only one you had entered as you might otherwise end up going all the way to the meeting and not get a ride.

The other side of the coin is that if you do enter and are accepted and don't turn up, you are obliged to inform the organizers of your reasons. You see, the fact of your being accepted may well mean that somebody else was refused – and *you* wouldn't like it, would you? And there are some types who enter more than one meeting on the same day to make sure of a ride and then choose which one they prefer on the day. That is, just for the record, an offence against the rules of the sport and you'll end up in trouble if you do it and get caught. It could be your licence on the line.

Most organizers will try to give at least one confirmed ride so the day won't be wasted but it has to be said that for the 1988 season there were plenty of spaces left vacant on many grids as many racers were feeling the financial pinch. An exception was, as usual, Brands Hatch, particularly the grand prix circuit on which everybody seems to want to ride in even four- and five-lap races.

So entering a club meeting is straightforward enough, things get slightly more complicated if you want to ride at national or restricted status meetings. For a start, if you want to ride at one of these it is you who have to obtain the regulations. They don't send them out to you, until you are well

A superb classic racing triumph. Good enough to get a press interview from the journalist. So do not forget the other type of paperwork. By supporting your sponsors in this way they will be more willing to support you in the future

enough known for *them* to invite *you* to enter. You will need to locate the organizers of the meeting, from the ACU Handbook or MCN Calendar, and write to the secretary requesting regulations. And when you do, make quite sure that you enclose a stamped addressed envelope.

The 'first come first served' system that applies to club events doesn't necessarily apply to national events because if there are more applications than spaces on the grid, the promoters will accept first those riders who have already established themselves and who are therefore likely to add lustre to the race programme. Don't forget, the organizers have to make a profit out of the meeting and spectators through the gate must be the first objective. The famous get chosen first.

A moment's thought about the business of organizing yourself for a busy season will soon bring the realization that you will be writing off for entry forms, getting others automatically and when you have an entry, getting entry passes and the final instructions with race numbers, etc.

With lots of letters, entry forms to be filled in and passes coming back, there is every chance of getting things nicely mixed up or forgotten. Some sort of system for keeping track of everything is

An enormous amount of paperwork goes into running any meeting. Officials here checking riders' licences as they sign on. And your potential insurance benefits are invalid if you don't

vital, planning is the name of the game. Draw up a list from the published calendar of meetings of those that you wish to ride at. Use it to record those you have already entered and the race number you have been allocated. Don't get passes for the various meetings mixed up either, you usually only get two or three per meeting. Your mates will have to pay to come and support you.

Insurance

Every time you enter a meeting a portion of the entry fee is insurance. It covers you for certain benefits if you are injured and off work but it really won't keep you in luxury. There's a scale for 'heavier' injuries too which although little enough reflects the fee and risk involved. It is possible to increase this insurance if you wish, through the ACU insurers and this address like others will be found on p. 125.

It is actually possible to insure your bike against crash damage though it really is expensive to the point where you wonder whether you couldn't repair the bike yourself for less. However, should you be running a big production bike costing £5000 + you might think it worth that expense, if you consider the cost of writing it off.

All this talk of insurance may create the thought that motorcycle racing is highly dangerous. Certainly it's the element of danger that makes it what it is and is part of the attraction. This kind of racing is, of course, dangerous as is almost any physical sport, but nowhere near as much as people suppose.

In 1986, the Government Office of Population Census and Surveys published a table of deaths in various sports. Top of the table were air sports with 18 fatalities, equal second were equestrian and ball sports (14) followed by mountaineering and rock-climbing (11), watersports and athletics (10). Then came motorcycling (8) and automotive sports (3).

Having some 30 relatively competitive years behind me, of winning races and championships at club level, an Isle of Man Production TT win and while still competing at international level, to date the injuries have been few: a broken elbow, bruises, the odd scar and one minor touch of concussion.

In many ways motorcycle racing is as dangerous as you choose to make it. Natural talent helps somewhat, but a studied approach to the subject will both minimize the risks and speed your progress relatively safely.

8

Getting on to the grid

You will never quite forget the first time you take your place on the grid, it's a magic moment. However, just like riding your bike on the road, you also need a licence to ride on the track: a competition licence.

Similarly, you have to apply to the licensing authority for the necessary forms, in this case from the Auto Cycle Union, see p. 125 for the address. It has to be said that you cannot dodge this bit of paperwork, since you will have to produce your licence each time you 'sign on' at a meeting. You cannot actually get out on to that place on the grid until you have completed the formalities that ensure that you, and everybody else associated with a race meeting, are insured for the day. And you cannot complete an insurance policy until you sign it!

One of the forms that you will receive is for a special medical examination, and that you can get from your local doctor. Unfortunately, it will be a private medical and you will therefore have to pay his fee. If you think about it, making sure that you are fit to compete in a hazardous sport is hardly a bad idea. For instance, it is possible that you might

be colour blind. If you were, then it is possible that you might mistake a marshall's flag signal. When these are explained later on, you will see that it could be as much for your own protection as it is for others.

While it is a condition that you have to join a club as part of the procedure to obtain your licence, you will want to join a club that stages meetings at your local circuit anyway. Club addresses are listed in the appendices so that you can find out who to write to.

Having joined the appropriate club, you have to get the secretary's signature on your licence application form to complete the formalities and now with that and the medical certificate complete and your fee enclosed, the ACU will send you your

---

A typical crowded grid before the action starts; butterflies are circulating in riders' stomachs but it's where every aspiring spectator would want to be

The grid gets away at Oulton Park in 1985 with Roger Marshall (no. 11) riding for Honda Britain leading Paul Lewis on the Skoal Bandit Suzuki (no. 44) and Ron Haslam (no. 5)

licence on receipt of them. You now have your novice licence and may ride at club meetings only.

Now novice riders have to wear a red jacket, you may have wondered when watching races what the significance was, it is simply so that other riders are alerted to your inexperience and give a little extra room when passing, a bit like an 'L' plate. The ACU will send you one of the regulation jackets, if you wish, for a small deposit. Alternatively, you can wear your own if you have one.

Before leaving basic requirements, there is one more before you can get on to that hallowed strip of tarmac, wherever it may be. You are also required to wear an identity disc, this is worn around the neck. It should have your name and date of birth on it; also recommended is your blood group. You could ask your doctor to check this when you have your examination.

The reason for the 'dog tag' is simply that if there are several riders taken from the circuit in one day to the local hospital, it will avoid any confusion. In a real emergency, your blood group could be pretty useful as well. Where can you buy your dog tag? In

a wide variety of sources, from jewellers to the local pet shop, and both can no doubt arrange the necessary engraving.

I'm sure that you would like to get rid of that red jacket just as soon as possible and the prescribed routine is that it has to be worn by a novice rider until he has raced at three different circuits and in ten separate meetings. As you do so you will collect the necessary evidence to that effect by going to the race administration and getting the secretary of the meeting to sign your licence in the spaces provided. Once having completed this routine, and it takes some riders just a couple of months and others a whole season, you send your licence back to the ACU who will upgrade it to a restricted licence at no extra cost. Now you can get rid of that jacket.

The next stage in your racing career is to start

Above Ron
Haslam with
Brian Fancourt;
Brian noting Ron's
critique of a rider's
technique

Left A grid of
classic racing
machines at
Snetterton where
champion of the
1960s Hugh
Anderson is still a
favourite on any
grid

Above **Almost any machine can be used for racing and here are a couple of Mini-stocks, stripped down Yamaha 250 LCs which provide good, cheap racing**

Left **Phil Read on a John Player Norton waits with other riders before being allowed on to the grid**

racing towards your national status licence. This is achieved by competing in ten races in separate meetings, on four circuits, and doing so in the first half of the field. Again, the secretary of the meeting will sign your licence to this effect but already you can see that you now have your foot on the first step of the racing ladder. The real no-hopers will not progress beyond this stage to higher levels of competition.

This is the first stage of a filtering process so that riders of very differing abilities do not compete together, thus increasing the hazards. Now you will be able to apply for and be the proud possessor of that national licence. The next step is rather more difficult, now you have to start scoring points towards an international licence.

When you get on to the grid at a national meeting, you earn your racing points by finishing in the first ten places: 6 for being in the first three; 4 from fourth to seventh; and 2 from eighth to tenth. The Manx Grand Prix is a special case because competing on the toughest course in the world gets the first 12 placed men 5 points, 13th to 20th earn 3

and even finishing earns 1. But believe me it's well earned, the course is nearly 38 miles round.

The object of the exercise for national licence holders is to accumulate 30 points during the previous two seasons, at which stage you can again apply to the ACU to be upgraded, for your international licence. Now you really can mix with the top class racers.

Now you can easily see that the riders who hold that status of licence have really earned their spurs. The system is a most effective filter of ability but even so, such is the difference in ability between the riders at the front and those at the back of the field, that those who just manage to get on to an international grid by making the cut on the qualifying time (another filter of ability) will be something like a mobile traffic jam to the more competitive riders in international races.

It is also worth noting that once having earned an international licence you have to continue to qualify for one. To renew one a rider needs to have gained at least one world championship point, or Eurochampionship point in the previous two years. Alternatively, he must have gained 20 points in the past three seasons at international meetings.

There is also something called a 'one day' international licence, which permits holders of a national licence, who have scored 15 points, to apply for a one day licence for up to two international events in one season.

So next time you watch a top international event and see the rider being lapped at the back of the field, remember that he's not quite the wally you might think. He has had to earn the right to be out there, and it wasn't that easy. Such is the difference between those who have developed the ability to be front-runners, and the 'nearly men' who nevertheless still have a lot of experience behind them.

Racing schools

If you are undecided about whether to fork out a lot of money on all the necessary equipment for racing, there is a way of getting a taste of it without commitment. Enrol on a course at a racing school.

There are currently two such schools operating, Knockhill and Brands Hatch. These provide both the opportunity to try your hand at the sport without the expense of using your own bike and racing kit, if you have them, and also to obtain the advice of an expert on your racing potential.

Above **Scene from the Brands Hatch Racing School, as a queue of would-be racers wait to follow the instructor on a conducted lap. Correct trackcraft is vital for a decent grid position**

Above right **Grand prix star Ron Haslam runs a master class at Donington for established racers wanting to improve; he compares notes here with a pupil**

For those who are not committed to a full-scale try at racing and wish to see if they would like it, there is much to recommend this approach. The advice of the school expert can also be the answer to problems of those not doing too well at the game and who seek advice on why they are finishing nearer the back of the field than the front.

The way these schools operate is to provide all the necessary equipment, leathers and helmet if you should need them. Perhaps more to the point, they also provide a bike upon which to make your debut on the tarmac. More valuable than sheer currency, though, is advice.

This is the way they operate: they will first assemble a group of riders in a classroom situation where an experienced racer will give a talk on the circuit and how it should best be approached – what speed, what gear for which corner, etc.

Then follows the practical side of the course. At Brands Hatch this will consist of several laps in convoy behind the instructor who will show the

correct lines and braking-points for each corner. After this the riders will be let loose to circulate on their own while instructors observe their performance and mark them accordingly. Having compared notes and stop watches, they will be in a position to give an educated opinion of the potential abilities, and shortcomings, of riders and can then offer advice on how to improve racetrack performance.

The Knockhill operation is similar, first there are briefings on trackcraft, followed by six lap sessions at which assessment takes place. These schools provide, above all, the opportunity to sample much of the experience of track racing but since there are far fewer riders on the circuit it will be under more controlled, and therefore safer, conditions.

If you want to try your hand without going in at the deep end, here are the addresses you need:

Brands Hatch Racing School
Freepost
Fawkham
Dartford
Kent DA3 8NG
Tel: 0474 872 367

Knockhill Motorcycle Racing Club
Knockhill Racing Circuit
Nr Dunfermline
Fife KY12 9TF
Tel: 0383 731788

9

Riding techniques

World champions are born, not made. However, it is also true that sheer dedication can take you a long way and build an ordinary talent into something to be respected. However, there are a lot of riders with ability who never seem to quite make it, perhaps time taken to analyse their abilities and a reasoned approach to the subject just might supply the missing element.

Those born with sheer talent have a natural ability that shines through, so easily recognized that you'll spot the guy at the front of the field after half a dozen races, given, of course, reasonable machinery.

The rest of us mortals gain hard earned experience over the seasons and gradually learn the ropes and hone what natural, fairly ordinary abilities we have. But even at club level there is only one champion per class. What follows is a distillation of experience gained over a generation or more of competition, a TT win, numerous championships and many of those while having passed the half century mark, but with the knowledge that I had a fairly average amount of talent.

Racing is such an adrenalin-generating pastime that many racers seldom get beyond the scramble-round-each-corner-as-fast-as-possible-without-falling-off stage, analysing what they are about is the last thing that comes to mind. Nevertheless, a little science applied really can produce results.

Science tells us that there is just one fastest line through any given corner, the line in fact that makes the greatest radius. True enough, the further you lay the bike over, the slower you have to go before

Another grid of 40-odd riders gets away at a club meeting at Snetterton. Push-starting is very much still the way they do it. 'Run and bump' needs to be mastered

flying off into orbit. Naturally the reverse is true. So the line of greatest radius through any corner is the fastest, right? Wrong. Racing in many instances is not an exact science, neither for that matter is motorcycle engineering, yet.

There will certainly be occasions when the seemingly obvious line through a corner may not be the fastest. Perhaps the track has ripples in the surface, it may be broken up right on the racing line therefore disturbing the bike and would be worthwhile avoiding. It may be a combination bend in which entering the first bend at a different position gives you a better run at the second part. Riding through the second part faster gets you into the straight faster and that means more mph down it.

It's worth noting here that a good rider on a relatively slow machine can actually pass a rider on a faster bike down the straight just by making a perfect exit from the previous bend. The physically faster machine, having exited the bend at a slower speed, will take longer to reach its top speed whereas the slower bike, having had a better run into it, will for the first part actually be travelling faster, and pass it. There's no truer saying in racing

than a tuner's best gimmick is a good rider.

Another instance when the 'fastest' line may actually be slower in the final analysis, is when approaching a corner in the ideal position a fellow competitor sneaks up the inside line. He will then block your line so that even if he were actually slower through it, you would not be able to pass him and in any case he'd get the better run into the straight, starting from in front of you.

But before the actual race, the start. The majority of races these days are started by the traffic light system, not all though – the Union Jack still rules at many club meetings. So if this applies to yours, well here is where the race could be won or lost. Watch several race starts to spot the flag waver's technique. Study the action: does the starter tense up visibly before bringing the flag down? Does he hold the flag aloft for a moment and is the time always the same? Perhaps he brings it straight up and down. Whatever the style, familiarity with it may give you the chance to get on the move at the first possible opportunity short of actually 'jumping the start'.

If it's a production bike then starting is pretty straightforward. Certainly if yours is a push-button job there shouldn't be a problem but it's still possible to polish the technique to get up with the winners. If you set the throttle so that it's a shade too wide then dropping the clutch with the motor already revving hard will probably produce a wheelie and you may need to back it off. Another possibility is that the motor may well not pick up immediately and again cost precious moments.

The throttle set just off the stop is probably the best setting but the tension generated on the grid often defeats your best intentions so if you happen to be unsure of your ability to keep the setting just right practice starting, establish the best throttle position and apply a spot of paint across the casing and the rubber. You'll then know it's exactly right.

Open class competitors usually have to push start; run alongside the bike, drop the clutch and bump the seat to get the motor to fire up. However, the trend seems to be moving to clutch starts as in Formula 1 or 500 grand prix races. Nevertheless, push-starting prevails right now and certainly can pose problems.

Once more the vital bit is to get the throttle setting spot on but while you are pushing as fast as physically possible it is difficult to keep it just right. This often means you open the throttle too wide and choke the motor or perhaps on a big four-stroke, lock the rear wheel. On a big machine it can be worthwhile setting the motor on a fastish tickover with the throttle against the stop, then when dropping the clutch you can usually be assured of the motor firing up.

While the race can certainly be won or lost on the startline, the approach to the first corner can be as vital. Watch a few starts and spot the rider who is flat on the tank as soon as the bike is moving and goes into that corner at race speed. Many seem to take a few moments to get comfortable before really switching into race mode. Some need half a lap before they can switch on the aggression. Race winners don't.

Above right In conditions like this 'wet' tyres would be used to cut their way through the water

Left The start of another Superstocks race; a national series based closely on road bikes with limited tuning and road chassis

Sometimes the biggest problem is simply that of your position on the grid. Being on the last row of a grid, perhaps eight rows deep, can ruin your chances before you even start. If you get boxed in at the back at the start of a race and the potential winner is on the front line, in a short six-lap club race your chances are somewhat dramatically reduced.

Some riders seem to be able to weave their way through the initial traffic with a skill never mastered by many. Certainly, when you get around 40 machines weaving about in front of you it's a pretty daunting sight and the need to dive into the middle and try and find a way through is something that some will never quite come to terms with.

You can, however, make the best of any situation on the grid with a little foresight. You may remember certain machines and riders as being slow starters and know that you simply have to set yourself to pass them if they happen to be right in front on the grid. If it's a newcomer who has to push a large, heavy four-stroke, then there's a good chance he'll block your way.

It may be the case that your club publishes the grid row you start from in the programme. In this case you have the chance to place yourself behind a quick starter if you happen to spot one. It can also give you the opportunity to try your chance to rush down the outside from a rear grid position, if you get on to the grid before most of the others.

Races are won and lost perhaps more at the first corner than anywhere else, simply because everybody on the grid will be trying to get round it at the same time. The possibilities for either gaining

Right Even if you miss your line through a corner all may not be lost. It is perfectly possible to recover, provided you keep your head

Below These classic riders splash their way through the puddles. When riding in these conditions try to be as smooth as possible

Keith Heuwen personifies the sort of determination that makes a successful racer. Here Heuwen is pictured at the Powerbike International in 1986

a lead, because the only potential winner is shut in behind them, or, grabbing the chance to catch him up with a demon overtaking move that gets you around the opposition in one move of pure opportunism, means everything in a six-lap scratch.

Certainly the first corner is the most difficult to take flat out simply because while it's not difficult to estimate your best approach speed when into the race, doing it the first and perhaps only time that day is certainly not so easy. It is also the place for more mistakes than at any other point in the race so a 'balls out' approach in the middle of the pack will probably get you into trouble.

The first corner is the place for opportunism; you may be boxed in, or away to a flyer, so may the rest of the competition. Making the best of whatever grid position you have drawn, elbowing your way through the pack, rushing right round the outside of the pack, or forgetting that the tyres are cold and overdoing it because it went sideways when you weren't expecting it, that first bend is crucial.

Braking

With many machines having similar performances these days, perhaps more races are lost on braking than most other situations. If you can get into a corner first, even if the other guy is faster round it, you may well be obstructing him. It is then difficult for him to pass you if you are on the racing line.

So, if you can develop a late-late-braking technique successfully, it certainly won't do you any harm. If you have been bombing down a long straight and almost get up to the machine's top speed, you'd probably be surprised just how hard you can grab the front brake lever before the wheel starts to skid. A little experimentation when you can find a spare bit of track by yourself will prove the point.

When you have learned to use the front brake really hard and if your bike has got the sort of anchors found on almost any racing bike or sports roadster, then you'll probably either have the rear wheel just about in contact with the road, or indeed,

right off the ground. A sort of reverse front-wheel wheelie.

The essence of late braking is accurate gauging of the point at which to apply them. Find some sort of marker to help you judge just where that point is. If you get outbraked at that point, either his brakes are better than yours, or he's just got more bottle.

However, the real braking that grabs the extra yard or two is not just in a straight line, that's easy enough. It's gauging the amount of braking you can do as you start to lay the bike into the corner with the brakes still on. This is hardly recommended while you are still learning the game and is easily the cause of a spill when miscalculated. But it's certainly what the quick men will be doing.

It's a technique that you will develop, of gradually letting the pressure off the lever the further over you lay the bike, until over as far as you dare, to

Above **There are actually three bikes in this picture taken at Donington, and if you compete at top level this is how close you ride**

Above right **American Kevin Schwantz and Aussie Paul Lewis duel on Suzukis**

the point where it's all off and you are almost at the apex of the bend. Then you blend the opening of the throttle with letting off the last bit of pressure and accelerate smoothly away so that the power is applied progressively as you exit the corner.

Cornering

It is natural to take a line into a corner from the outside of the track, crossing the apex and then out to the edge again: the greater the curve you can

strike the faster the potential speed. Trying to out-brake an opponent puts you into the position of blocking his line into a corner, given that you are trying to get alongside on the *inside* of the line he has chosen. If you both hold your lines you will be right on the apex with him outside you and that's the place to be. On the outside he has to travel further and faster to overtake, and it may well be that travelling as fast as you can, *your* line towards the outside of the track will mean he has to let you go.

Now if that is interpreted as deliberate obstruction, then it's less that than a fact of life on the track. Competition is so close that this is a classic situation in which you will frequently find yourself. Whether you are both trying to hold on until the last moment on braking or beat each other round a corner, in the final analysis it's down to your own intestinal fortitude as to who gives way first.

In the situation just outlined, often the man on the inside would modify his line just enough to let the other man go for it and exit a little tighter than you would otherwise, and you both go into the straight side by side. You don't actually want to bash fairings, do you? It's getting closer to the first aid post than many would want, however, some are determined enough to try almost anything. Some come unstuck.

Cornering is, of course, what it's all about. There are many kinds of manoeuvres and tactics that are all part of the fun and make you more competitive but in the final analysis, it's the fastest rider round the bends that wins the day. You may well be slower than many when you make your debut but improvement is usually possible.

Today's tyres, even road tyres, provide incredible grip when used to the maximum by an expert; watch a national production championship race. It

is all about sharpening your sense of judgement on how far over you can lay the bike while still accelerating. In other words, spot the moment when the rear wheel starts to slide.

Continually riding round the same corner means trying that little bit harder each time until the time when you think you're on the limit and a slide to disaster the next move. Well, unless you are already on your way to winning everything you enter, there will always be a time when you feel you are at maximum and somebody just drives around the outside of you.

It is somewhat ego deflating but if you do go racing, deflated it will frequently be, but don't be disheartened. Practice, practice, practice. I've known some riders who did little enough for several years but suddenly found the motivation to go that bit quicker to get into the winning groove. It took

Top left **On the limit – Richard Scott on Honda VFR slides round on his knee-pad to show just how far over it's possible to get**

Above left **Works Heron Suzuki in full flight. Older versions of this Suzuki two-stroke four-cylinder 500 can be found at club events. It has now been superseded by a V4 version**

Above **This scrap at Oulton Park led to rider no. 10, Tony Head, biting the dust as he starts to 'high side' into the scenery**

me seven years to actually win my first race and although I did manage to set the odd lap record on the way, I didn't get beyond second spot.

Slipstreaming

The next guy's bike may be that bit quicker than yours but all is not lost as slipstreaming may be the answer. If you can get close enough to the bike in front of yours, with perhaps barely a yard between you, it can be worth another five miles per hour on your top speed as his faster machine punches a hole through the atmosphere for you to follow in. You will literally be sucked along in his slipstream.

This is where tactics really come into play. It may be that you have been in front and he passes you down the straight. Or you may have worked your way through the field to get up behind him coming into a corner. Either way, the aim is to nip closely into his slipstream and get a tow. Beware though, if you are swerving into somebody's slipstream as they pass you, make sure there isn't some-body already doing the same thing. Otherwise you might be heading for the first aid post again.

The object of the exercise is, of course, to be in a position to come out of his slipstream and nip in front on the last lap at the last corner before the end of the race. Doing so before could mean that with your opponent's better top speed he will simply pass you back. So if you do get in behind somebody don't be in too much of a hurry to pass, or repass. You can actually beat the faster machine – if you use your head.

Harassment

An odd word to use in the racing context. Nevertheless, there's no better description for this technique. It's the best way of pressurizing an opponent into making a mistake.

You may be evenly matched with an opponent to the point where, if he happens to be in front, there's no way you can ride round or outbrake him; it's that close. You will just keep riding round together, unless you can devise a plan to break the impasse. It's possible.

The 'game plan' is to get your front wheel almost alongside anywhere you can whether you believe you can pass or not. Continually showing him your front wheel at every opportunity going into a corner, or just peeling off into one, will really keep the pressure on. The continual harassment can sometimes force a mistake if his nerves aren't quite as strong as yours – and after all, that's what it's all about.

Traffic

Dicing your way through a field, or even lapping backmarkers when you are involved in a dice, can offer chances to gain advantage if you can just work it right. Waiting a moment before passing a slower man going into a corner can leave a pursuing rider no chance to follow you through. It can be the only way to shake somebody off who is trying to harass you into a mistake. Timing is the key.

The last corner

So often races are won and lost on the last corner before the finish. Close club racing frequently produces that sort of finish and one more bit of thought at the critical moment can turn defeat into victory.

Trying to pull out of an opponent's slipstream to nip by just before the flag quite often doesn't come off, simply because there is not enough time to make the manoeuvre work. It can, however, be enhanced quite effectively. Instead of going into that corner as close behind the other guy as possible, try hanging back a few yards going in so that you can get a clear run and really go for it. When coming out and travelling that little bit faster, running up his slipstream at the same time, gives something of a slingshot effect and may be just enough to win the day as you pull out in time to take the flag first.

Schwantz and Rainey fight it out. Suzuki and Honda go for it at Brands Hatch as they powerslide their Superbikes

10

Plan your way to the top

In a very long racing career, I've seen so many racers come and go. Some made it, some didn't. Some succeeded yet had limited talent, others, talented, won lots of club races yet disappeared from the scene after just a season or two, giving up for a variety of reasons. Many just couldn't afford to continue racing at the financial level to which they had somehow become accustomed – perhaps two meetings every weekend of the season.

A careful selection of meetings can achieve several objectives. For instance, if you know from watching the race calendars that a busy weekend is coming up with several meetings to choose from and perhaps a round of some championship or other in the class which you happen to be racing, then entering a small club meeting at which there will therefore be rather less competition, will enhance your chances of a win. Good stuff for that dossier which you will be preparing to show the potential sponsor.

You can see, therefore, that it's possible to magnify a lesser talent by gaining what may look on paper to be a good track record. Championships are a pretty useful statistic to have in your portfolio and these can often be won simply by making sure of a reasonable performance at all the meetings that the club holds. If the club holds meetings at several widely dispersed circuits then you can be sure that most members just won't bother to participate in them all so that your accumulated points can better the guy who normally beats you, but doesn't race at all the meetings.

Making the most of your meagre financial resources has to be a good idea yet lack of planning is something many are guilty of considered in the light of an overall planned racing career. As I have shown, it is possible to become a big fish in a small pond, costing lots of time and money, yet the effort may well go largely unnoticed. It's an easy trap to fall into, finding a local circuit you go well at, you tend to get to like success and keep on going there. Making the effort and commitment to travel far and wide and certainly initially getting blown off by the local hero is hardly satisfying but it is the way to progress, building up your total experience and circuit knowledge.

I'll say it again; racing is an ego trip. It's about getting yourself noticed. Enough attention, from the media anyway, can be the way to unlock doors and opportunities. It's the first guy past the post who gets noticed, and where you won't is by choosing to ride in a race that combines several classes, but in overall terms leaves you at a disadvantage. Like riding a 250 cc bike in a combined class production race, for instance, or combined class four-stroke events. You may win your classification, but nobody besides your mates is likely to know.

Before you send in your membership cash to join a club, make sure they run a race, and preferably a championship class, for your chosen machine. Some clubs run separate events for 250 cc production bikes, even up to 500 cc, or singles up to 500 cc. Spot the opportunity to plan your maximum potential exposure.

The Isle of Man is a good stepping-stone up the ladder to stardom and whether it's just the challenge of competing on the world's toughest course, or

Ex-world champion Phil Read with the famous Team Obsolete Matchless G50 from the USA. Phil has made something of a comeback by competing in classic events like many another old racer. Indeed, age is no barrier to the rewards of motorcycle sport

whether you deliberately set out to win the new-comers' race in the Manx Grand Prix, it's still got enough kudos to make a good result worthwhile. Good enough to justify a separate chapter.

Naturally, you will want to progress as fast as possible and in the process of upgrading your licence a little planning can speed things up. Find a club, or combination, that gives the circuit opportunities you require. And in order to make sure that you finish far enough up the field to qualify for another signature on your licence you could, perhaps, be more selective in your choice of event – you don't have to enter the toughest one.

So the lesson in this chapter is to plan. Check which class gives you the best chance, which meetings will do your career the most good, and do so for the coming season in advance. Make a plan and set objectives. When the season is over look back on it and see how you can profit from it to make the next one better. The best plan may not simply be winning as many races as possible.

Above **How not to start, no. 11 has 'dialled' up too many revs and just dropped the clutch in his haste. Practice your starting technique**

Right **Salute the victors. Victorious Americans at the 1987 Transatlantic Trophy meeting. The feeling is the same even when you come out top in your first club event**

11

Racing in the Isle of Man

Events in the Isle of Man still have quite enough impact on the UK scene to make it a worthwhile stepping-stone to success. A good result, for instance, in the Manx Grand Prix, can earn plenty of kudos and recognition. TT success can bring all sorts of rewards such as contracts to ride in nationally known teams.

For me, the TT course is the supreme road racing challenge, indeed so many want to race there that it can be very difficult to even get an entry, so oversubscribed are some of the races. However, since they introduced a newcomer's race into the Manx Grand Prix programme and opened up the class limit to 1300 cc, it has allowed many to make their debuts on a big production bike, and relatively inexpensively at that.

The fascination of the island is, of course, its sheer length. If you spent your formative motor-cycling years on the roads and enjoy the challenge of a fast, winding road going at speed, then the Isle of Man is a most enjoyable experience which combines the best of that with being able to use all the road. It is a unique road racing experience.

In many ways, racing there is not actually racing, it's a time trial. Often the only fellow competitor you'll see is the one you initially shared the grid with, as the start of a race in the island is in pairs at ten-second intervals. Even when practising with some 300 competitors on the track at the same time, you can go for miles before you overtake, or get overtaken. It can actually seem quite lonely compared to the hectic hurly-burly of short circuit six-lap dashes.

Riders in the island start off in pairs at ten-second intervals as a mass start would be too dangerous. This pair are going to start a practice lap

This is not the place for the cut and thrust of short circuit racing, a completely different mental attitude is required. The 'go for it' hard charging approach is not the way to get a good lap time. This always seems to come when you relax and adopt the laid-back method. A smooth, unhurried approach when you take time to get the lines just right and develop a rhythm will get you the result when you least expect it.

Racing in the island does pose some problems in setting up the bike. Factors that have to be borne in mind are that the motor will spend much longer on full throttle, the suspension will have more to cope with in travelling over humps and bumps at the bike's maximum speed and also the brakes will get heavier and more sustained use in some sections.

In the first instance it may be that a compression ratio with which the motor can cope quite happily on a short circuit, will be too high when on full load for a couple of miles or pulling hard going up the mountain. Pre-ignition and piston failure can therefore be an unexpected problem and if the

liberal use of Avegas, available on the island, will not cure it then a lowering of the compression ratio is the only alternative. If you are only going for a finish then lowering it before you go at the expense of performance might be useful insurance.

Suspension, too, can be a problem, usually resulting from the damping being unable to cope with extended high-speed travelling over the many humps and bumps around the 37 miles, fade is a distinct possibility. Consider a new standard rear unit on a production bike or a racing component on an open-class machine.

Suspension settings that were perfectly satisfactory on smooth, short circuits can be less than ideal in 'The Isle of Bikes'. Too hard setting on spring pre-load can bring problems with the damping coping with the rebound and consequent wobbling as the unit 'tops out' and the rear wheel skips over bumps. Less pre-load and more damping is the answer both for a softer ride and better roadholding over bumps.

Most of the places where heavy braking is required leave enough time for everything to cool down before the next application but coming down the mountain can produce fade due to over-cooked linings and fluid boiling. This usually occurs after heavy braking first at the Creg, then Brandish, followed by Signpost and Governor's. It is probable that your standard racing linings will do the job but harder grade may be necessary.

Learning the circuit is most of the battle for any newcomer and it is possible to speed up the process before you even get there. There are videos of the circuit of rather high-speed tours by people like Joey Dunlop in *Vee for Victory* or a similar one done by Mick Grant. Unfortunately the Dunlop one is so fast that unless you already know something of the circuit it becomes meaningless. The Grant version though was made with him using a Suzuki Katana and is therefore much slower, but for your purposes much more useful.

An alternative that can work for some is to spend time studying an Ordnance Survey map of the circuit. Try listing all the names that you can find on the map, then get a friend to test you by throwing you the name of a corner; try and remember the

Close dicing through Parliament Square. It is so slow through here that mistakes are frequently made by trying too hard

one that comes before and after. And if you do have some idea of what sort of a bend it is, you will start to form a picture that will quickly come alive when you get there. When you see the name come up on the signboard preceding the corner, you'll remember what's coming up next that much quicker.

Of course, there is no substitute for lapping the course as often as possible. To further this end, many riders take a road bike as well and use it to get laps in while the roads are open to the public, at legal speeds obviously; the local police are frequently vigilant. Riders using their production bikes often use them out of practice sessions to get miles in on the course, but don't forget the insurance, the roads are public.

When riding the course itself, the speeds achieved by the experts will seem astronomic until you start to realize just how many sections there are that can be taken flat out, or very near it on many bikes.

Above **Ramsey Hairpin in the rain – down to 15 mph as Phil Mellor leads Joey Dunlop, but he was to slide off**

Opposite **Production racing in the island has produced some of the best and closest racing ever and this group sweeping through Signpost Corner and down to Bedstead are a good example**

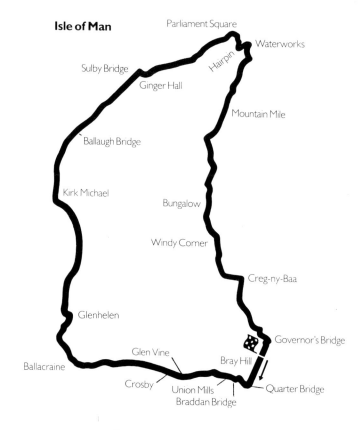

Isle of Man

Parliament Square
Waterworks
Hairpin
Sulby Bridge
Ginger Hall
Mountain Mile
Ballaugh Bridge
Kirk Michael
Bungalow
Windy Corner
Creg-ny-Baa
Glenhelen
Governor's Bridge
Glen Vine
Bray Hill
Ballacraine
Crosby
Union Mills
Quarter Bridge
Braddan Bridge

Here is a brief description of the course, to illustrate the point:

From the start down through Bray Hill to Quarter Bridge can be taken at high speed, these days, indeed flat out on most bikes, when you have got used to the idea.

Quarter Bridge is almost a silly sharp corner because it seems so slow, but beware, somebody always falls off there, usually accelerating out and finding the camber drops away, and it's often on the first lap when the tank is full. The secret is to use every bit of road on the left before peeling off.

The sprint down to Braddan is a real 'bang it through the gears' job, the trick lies in spotting where to brake and peel off. You run up to Braddan through a slight right/left curve and the trick is to aim for the right-hand kerb and wait for the

chequers on the kerb to appear, peeling off some yards before they start.

The speed out of Braddan Bridge is largely determined by the drive through the right-hand part over the railway bridge. To get this right, position the bike almost against the railings on the left-hand side of the road before peeling off.

The bends that follow Braddan can be ignored, in other words take the obvious racing lines and just drive through. You can keep the throttle open until the approach to Union Mills. This is a pretty straightforward right/left downhill with the only complication being the ripples on the road on the way out at the apex on the left. If you get the drive out right, it can mean saving time on the long climb up to Glen Vine village.

The right-hander after the entry into the village is one where time can be made. It is straightforward

enough but is a real test of nerves, you may just need to back it off a shade, or even knock it down a gear on a Superbike.

Running down into Crosby village there's a gentle left-hand curve which at around 150 mph looks like a bend but for racing purposes is not. It's another test of nerves but in fact the whole section from the top of the hill at Glen Vine right through to Greeba Castle should be taken with all the strain that you can get on the throttle wire.

Greeba Castle is simple enough, a left/right. However, it's on the entry that time can be made, keeping the throttle open right into the left-hander on the way in and running up the hill after the Highlander, before knocking it back at least one gear.

The Appledene section that follows is high-speed swervery along the way through to Greeba Bridge. When you know that section you will be surprised when you find yourself cracking through the left/right/right.

Greeba Bridge is a left-hander where, if you use the chequers on the right-hand curve to peel off by, it all comes right. Now you can go for it again and get it right and accelerate all the way through to Ballacraine, but it does require a fair bit of bottle on an 1100 cc bike.

Ballacraine is faster than you would at first think. A right-hander where the commentator might well announce your progress to the listening thousands around the island, and indeed, Manx Radio covers quite a bit of the northern mainland as well.

Now for the most difficult section on the course, from Ballacraine through to Glenhelen Hotel, probably the last one that you will really be sure of. It's swervery all the way and even less forgiving than the rest of the circuit. Even so, it's still fast when you know it, but don't take liberties until you do.

Up the road from Ballacraine towards Ballaspur the hump at the top of the slight climb can be taken really hard if you get it right, swerving left then right and on down to Doran's Bend, which goes round the white wall of the house that you will see as you now rocket downhill.

Doran's is, again, rather faster than it looks and there's little to upset a bike that handles well so it's on up the road towards Laurel Bank, but first, a sharp downhill right/left before it comes into view. There's a trick to getting Laurel's right-hander sorted, it's simply getting far enough over to the left to get it lined up so that you can drive all the

Above **Triumph Daytona rounds Creg-ny-Baa to win the 500 cc production race in 1968 with Ray Knight aboard. He still campaigned a similar machine in the classic Manx Grand Prix in 1988**

Right **The ess bend through Braddan Bridge shows the crowds that gather on every vantage point for the races. Author testifies that those bales are very hard – or they were in 1973**

way through and come out fast with road to spare. Try actually running up the white line marking the edge of the road, on the left-hand side of the road, there really is room to spare.

Rushing up the gradual climb now to the garage at the 9th Milestone, the way to get through the very fast left/right into Black Dub is to drive right up to the kerb at the beginning of the garage forecourt, peeling off in short circuit style and driving hard through – don't get it wrong, try it gradually faster each time.

To try and guide you through the next bit 'off the page', is difficult. Take it at your own best judged speed, sweeping from side to side of the road before arriving at the right-hander before the Glenhelen Hotel. Here the bridge juts out into the road and you have to be really close to it before driving sharp left up the hill in front of the hotel.

The climb up from Glenhelen Hotel is a sharp one to Sarah's Cottage. The only difficult part of what is simply a right-hander is that the approach is difficult, having to cross the camber, coupled with, in the wet, the fact that there are frequently slippery patches around left by the leaves which they do try to clear before races. It's the place where Mike Hailwood and Giacomo Agostini both fell off in the Senior TT years ago, and it still catches some out now even though it's been smoothed over since then.

Greg Willies Hill which follows is pure Isle of Man magic. It's a case of throwing the bike from side to side as you accelerate up the hill and if you get it right even a very quick bike can be taken up there on the throttle, but like anywhere else in the island, there's little room for mistakes.

Up now on to the Cronk-y-Voddy Straight for another mile which you can take screwing it all on, even the right-hander at the end of the straight can be treated in cavalier fashion – it's just a question of bottle, then on down through right-handers to the 11th Milestone, known by the locals as Drink-waters Bend.

This very fast left-hander has a danger in the approach. If you got through the previous right-handers flat out you will probably be in the wrong place on the road to take the left-hander quickly, as indeed it can be taken. You'll probably knock it down one or even two gears for this one just for peace of mind but get it right and it's very fast indeed and where the aces make lots of time.

Handley's Cottage is next, a quarter of a mile after the 11th. It's just an ess, but with an obvious stone wall on the right at the entrance it's a bit off-putting. The guide is not to take perhaps the obvious entry point, in the right-hand gutter, but to go in around the white line because on the exit the camber drops away sharply, and in any case the object of the exercise is to tuck yourself right in under that wall as you power out.

One of the course's real features comes next; Barregarrow – pronounced by the locals as 'Bi'garrow'. It consists of two parts: the crossroads at the top of the hill, which is really very quick if you tuck the bike into the right-hand side of the road as you approach it, in fact it's almost flat on most bikes. The real test is in the second part driving steeply down the long hill towards the white wall at the bottom, around which the road curves. You positively rocket down that long hill and it's just a case

of where your nerve runs out. Brave types can get a medium fast machine through there flat, my Triumph Daytona Classic bike for the Manx Grand Prix is a positive delight at around 118 mph, and I'm straining every nerve to make it go faster. The GSX-R 1100 Suzuki really makes me bottle out around 8000, in top on standard gearing, say 130 mph.

The 13th Milestone which comes up next is a place where time can be gained, once you know it. After recovering from the rush down Barregarrow, it's hard right after dropping a gear and driving steeply downhill. The real key is the drive out, *very* hard left and here the time is made. Getting the drive on as you go down the hill is imperative and you will find the road opens out on the exit, indeed as do many bends on the island.

There's not too much to say about Kirk Michael, it is simply a right-hander but the houses and walls are real constraints to racing. Once you have bounced exhaust notes off the house walls on the way through the village, an experience to remember, Rhencullen comes next. This is just another long ess which can be taken at around 110–120 mph, which means one or two gears down

Dunlop between the dry stone walls on the works Rothmans' Honda VFR racer speeds to yet another win

depending on how brave you are.

The key here is to get the exit right and then you will gain speed for the run into an amazingly fast section through Bishop's Court. Here you will be driving hard in top gear on most machines going right to left in succession through bends until Alpine Cottage. This is only a fast right-hand curve but it's one you'll gradually learn to go faster and faster through on the run from Kirk Michael to Ballaugh.

After Ballaugh there are miles of flat out racing to come, making you appreciate why it's possible to average such high speeds. Everybody seems to have different ideas on how to take this famous jump. My own though, is simply that it's very hard on the bike to jump miles into the air and come down with a crunch and snatch on the transmission which could tax everything beyond safety limits. After all, if the rear wheel is not on the tarmac, it is not driving you forward, is it?

The next couple of miles are only interrupted by the leap over Ballacryre Rise, but is something you have got used to, leaping the bike over bumps at very high speeds. Take it flat in top and hang on with your teeth tightly gritted. And so on to Quarry Bends.

Steve Hislop heels into Signpost Corner in the Formula II race in 1987. Signpost is sharp right, in second or third gear, after some very hard braking

These are now mostly flattened right out and only the right/left on the way through gives thought for anxiety on a fast bike, then screw it up all the way through and down the long, and now very smooth, Sulby Straight. Once it was so bumpy that this alone limited the speed as the bike leapt from bump to bump and the bars went from lock to lock. Now it's one of the places where you can take a rest.

After something like a mile and a third with the throttle against the stop, braking is the only problem at Sulby Bridge's right-hander. You will find though that there are a couple of marker boards on the approach to assist judgement. Racing uphill now, Ginger Hall looks like a straightforward left-hander, but you do have to start from the right-hand gutter and cross the sharp camber twice as you sweep through. Caution under the trees when it is wet.

Following this, you have to drive over a series of bumps on the way up the succeeding short rise and these are sufficient to set the bike wobbling over irregularities. From the crest, the road then goes quite sharply down into Kerrow Moar. More bumps pose problems here, in what is a straightforward, though blind, left-hander. Braking downhill over the bumps causes some to lose control on the way in, so it can pay to go in a little slower and be able to get the power back on earlier to steady the bike up as you drive through the following

Above Pitlane – the lull
before the storm. Pits are
being prepared for a race
and all the refuelling
hoses are laid out. You
fill and empty your
allocated containers

Right Riders approach
Guthries' Memorial with
Ramsey in the back-
ground. A tight second or
third gear ess bend

Left This is the
copybook way of taking
Quarter Bridge's tight
right-hand corner and
Roger Marshall shows
how it is done. Adverse
camber on the way out

right-hander. Incidentally, exiting from this section you cross a sharp camber and the bike wheelies somewhat, but it's something you get used to.

The long bumpy run on to Glentrammon is another stretch where the average speed goes back up again and along here you can give any bike its head. There is a kink in the road at Glen Duff but it can be straightlined. Along here you may find out why a steering damper is useful, flat out over a series of ripples and bumps generated by tree roots under the road surface.

Glentrammon is a short, difficult section where

lots of time can be gained. This is particularly so on the approaching long left-hander through which it's possible to drive hard, though nerves suggest otherwise. Get it right and you don't have to slow down until you spot the marshall's post as you position the bike to go right and downhill. If you changed down at this point then going down another gear is probably right. The key to getting out of Glentrammon's left-hander fast is spotting the late peel-off point from the gutter on the right-hand side of the road, obvious to say, less obvious when you try it.

The run to Milntown Cottage is high-speed swervery all the way through as the road snakes from side to side and when learning you can do worse that just follow the road. Go on past the cottage and over the slight jump at the bridge and into Ramsey.

Parliament Square's only lesson is to make haste slowly. It really is quicker to slow right down almost to clutch-slipping speed if that's what you need to do to get the bike almost against the kerb on the apex of the sharp right-hander. It's actually quite a difficult discipline but standing the bike up as soon as you can to put the power on early and drive hard through the left-hander on the way out is what works for me. It also reduces the chances of a spill because don't forget that Parliament Square is a very busy public road and dampness can make it a skating rink.

May Hill is a short uphill blast and it is difficult because of those dreaded bumps again. Until the Highways Board sort it, it's the place where a simple double apex right-hander becomes the place where you wrestle with the bars to make the bike go where you want it. A well-handling machine really scores here and likewise through the following left.

Stella Maris's fast right follows, then comes the notorious Ramsey Hairpin, another place where you come down to silly speeds in normal racing terms. A slower speed pays again but the stretch up to Waterworks 1 is under the trees and it's where dampness hangs about even on fine days and where adhesion can be less than normal. Waterworks 1 is quite a fast right – just drop a gear, Waterworks 2

It may be primitive, but taking note of the message could mean a winning time

means hard braking and down another to go further right and up the climb towards the Gooseneck.

This is similar to Ramsey Hairpin in some ways but right instead of left, and steep uphill. Getting it right is the key to gaining speed up the steep climb that follows; simply brake right against the left wall, apex against the right bank and away skimming the spectators' legs dangling down from the slope. It is a good place to have a mate signalling your progress which he can often pick up from the public commentary. There is still time on the last lap to snatch a place as you go over the mountain.

Guthries' Memorial comes next and there's time to be gained on the way into the slow left/right. It's a place where you can drive all the way through what looks like a couple of lefts, but these can be blended into one and braking left quite late, with the machine upright, just before laying it into the first part of the ess.

There are no unusual features over the next couple of miles because it encompasses the Mountain Mile, the run up into it and then the flat right at the end into the Mountain Box. It's the place for slipstreaming much faster machines, so much so that it can pay to hang behind one just to gain the extra miles per hour that the tow will give you. It's also the place where really tucking in behind the fairing pays off. Watch the rev-counter as you stick an elbow out into the draft. And pulling a tooth lower gearing can pay off here too, simply because there's more to be gained on the long climb up Snaefel than a flash reading of another couple of hundred revs going downhill past the Highlander.

The two lefts that are the Mountain Box are taken as one, driving hard out as it's still quite a steep climb. There follows more typical swervery from side to side of the road almost impossible to describe in detail but taking you up to the Black Hut's very fast left then on into the Verandah.

You can hardly avoid the advice on the signboard as you hammer into this one hard in fourth or fifth, as it clearly says 'Four Bends'. They are all varying parts of what is one long right-hander if you can get the perfect line and speed to take it in one shot. When you crack it, it gives a terrific boost and you can be going so fast on the way out that you nick into top as you straighten up from being laid over a long, long way.

The run down to the Les Graham Memorial, or Bungalow Bridge, is slightly downhill and for the brave the long left is very quick indeed. Next, a sort of Verandah in reverse: four rights taken as one as you come up to the Bungalow, just a left/right ess taken over the electric railway lines. No point in trying to be a hero here, there's little time to be saved.

It's a long climb now up to Brandywell and the

Eddie Laycock lines up to take Creg-ny-Baa's sharp right-hander. In the background is Kate's Cottage and the steep run down the long hill poses severe strains on braking

straightforward left-hander is usually made difficult because the entry point is not obvious and the slight right-hand curve before puts you in just the wrong place for getting a good line through. Go in a bit slower to get right over to the right-hand side.

A little swervery now and then you come to the 32nd Milestone. This is one of the features of the course because there's a very sharp drop over the fence down the valley and the road looks particularly narrow from the speed you will reach. The three succeeding lefts can be blended into one taken really quickly if you can steel yourself to hang on late going in and keep the speed up. You can in fact take it so fast if you really do it right that I've been known to ground the prop-stand frame bracket on the Suzuki, others must have even more fun.

Down now into Windy Corner, what looks to be a 'go for it' right. On a good day it is, that is, when there isn't a strong wind blowing up the valley, which is the exception. This actually causes spills on occasion, picking the bike up at the critical moment, or even getting right under the bike to lift the front wheel.

The following 33rd Milestone is a real blinder in that the double apex left can be taken around 120–130 mph. There are no problems apart from sheer bottle and getting the entry right, which is up against the yellow chequered fence posts on the way in.

You are now starting the fast run down the mountain and in fact it's possible to push and coast all the way back to the start if a finish means that much to you and you are in trouble. Many manage to run out of fuel here on the last lap – I've done it too.

Carry on through Keppel Gate's sharp and slow left, down through the very bumpy left-hander at Kate's Cottage and on to the pub at Creg-ny-Baa. It's a long undulating descent, a real brake tester and while the Creg is simply a right-hander, it always catches somebody out, either on the exit, or on the persistent damp patch on the apex on all but the sunniest day.

The next stretch is probably the fastest part of the course, the mile down to Brandish's left-hander. There's time to tuck right down and check out the best reading on the rev-counter before crashing on the brakes again but be careful, they may still have hot fluid in the system from the Creg, or the pads may still be too warm, because it's 'all stop' from

Left Sidecars line up into Guthries. On the racing line there are three bends on the way in that all blend into one

Right Geoff Johnson demonstrates the style on his Loctite Yamaha that has taken him to race wins. Winners ride between those ragged walls at almost 'ten-tenths' short circuit effort; a style not to be adopted by the newcomer

your highest possible speed. To help, there is a warning marker-board on the left-hand side of the road going in to help you judge the distance. A good peeling-off point here is the gate into the field on the right-hand side of the road.

The course goes down again now towards Hillberry, with time to get back into top before the right-hander, very fast and nerve testing. It's the place where stars save lots of time and get a faster run up towards Cronk-ny-Mona. This is a very long left and if you can keep out over the white line before peeling off going in, it will get you into position to sweep through very fast before Signpost Corner comes up. Then it's braking again that poses the real problem.

Signpost is downhill going in and the sliproad there has proved to be useful as it's too easy to brake late, since there are few points that stand out to help you judge the corner. But the corner itself is straightforward enough, driving out hard and continuing down to Bedstead's left, entering it from the gutter on the right and driving almost round past the apex and going really hard on the way out.

The approach to The Nook is narrow and bumpy and late braking is not to be encouraged as there is

no room for error and the bumps are sufficient to upset the line through the quite tight right-hander. It is at this point as you go down the final drop into Governor's that the accumulated effects of successive braking may take their toll as this final and very hard application can be the last straw. Fortunately there's plenty of room to run wide.

There really isn't any time to be made through Governor's, it's so very slow, probably the slowest of all corners in racing. It's an acute right, then down into a left-hander tucking in tight to the wall in order to get a good drive out through the uphill right towards the start/finish. It's frequently damp here under the trees even on a warm day.

This is a sketchy itinerary outlining just the prominent points of the course. Learning just where it's safe to go fast on a fast bike will get in laps over what was the magic ton on a first visit, and that applied to something like a production 750. These days, 110 mph seems to be the target that says you've really cracked the island. Once you have, there is no greater satisfaction, for me, than completing the 37.7 mile course without a single mistake.

12

Endurance racing

Endurance racing is a branch of racing that flourishes on the Continent and indeed there was a world championship for the series up to 1988. As it happened there were several races staged in the UK for the 1987 season; a world championship round at Donington, the Pirelli Six Hours Championship of three rounds – Brands Hatch and two at Snetterton staged by Bemsee, plus the Bantam Club's Six Hours, also at Snetterton.

The international races are for endurance specification machines, to current Formula 1 rules. The others are for production class bikes and at club level so anybody can ride, though entries are sometimes limited. Although they are expensive to enter and wearing on machines and tyres, they are not actually dear when you consider just how much time each rider spends racing, and in any case it provides a degree of fun not found in any other way.

Endurance racing is first and foremost a team sport. For a start, in a six-hour event you have two riders, mechanics to fill you up and others to lap score. Efficient pitwork can save you precious time and the teamwork can actually beat teams who ride faster.

For 24-hour events, three riders are allowed but are not compulsory. The team of mechanics which changes wheels, brake pads and refuels, if nothing else, will also require catering for and housing and transporting considerable distances – since these events usually only take place on the Continent. Other ones may be 1000 kilometres or eight hours in duration.

The fascination of long-distance racing is that unlike a short event where it's often all over if you are passed out there, you have time to have a really long dice and in fact often wear down a rider who cannot sustain consistent lap times for any length of time. Stressing the team side of the game, frequently a pairing will be unequal with one quick rider and a somewhat slower partner, a consistent pair equally matched but slower than the aceman can beat them.

Machine preparation, too, is a vital part of the exercise and in, for example, six-hour racing there's many a minor mechanical failure that quickly remedied can still keep you in the hunt. If you wondered whether a bike wouldn't be somewhat shattered after hours of racing, a well-prepared production bike will now go the whole way through a six-hour event without needing a change of tyres or brakes on most circuits and will be very far from 'tired' in the engine room.

Certainly for those who tire of countless six-lap dashes and seek something more challenging and demanding and in which others can share a vital part, endurance racing holds very real attractions. Neither is it so very much slower either, machines will lap consistently just a second or so short of race winning times achieved by bikes in short races.

The camaraderie generated by a number of hours of, say, six people all working together to score a result is worth experiencing. It's a far cry from just the rider getting all the action and satisfaction and this aspect makes it a unique experience where all can really be involved.

For instance, lap scorers showing the time achieved on every lap to the rider out there is important. It's important for the rider so that he can see if he is maintaining consistent times or is slowing up and is not really aware of it.

Even more vital in terms of rider morale, perhaps, is the mere fact of being regularly 'talked to' and not succumbing to the feeling of isolation and just 'riding round', it keeps up the motivation when you are riding for an hour or so. Perhaps more obviously is the need to be kept informed of how you are progressing with regard to the opposition. Races

Above Pitstops are vital in endurance racing and here one of the Rothman's Hondas is refuelled; the fuel lines have spring-loaded valves that automatically open and close as they are applied to the petrol tank. Stops take just seconds

Left The author in the 1986 Bol d'Or 24 Hours race, the annual 24-hour classic

Left The packed stands at the start of the Bol d'Or as the riders line up for the sprint across the track. The atmosphere is absolutely electric

Below left Britain, too, has its endurance races. In 1987 there were four, including the three rounds of the Pirelli Six Hours Championship. Here a Snetterton event gets under way

Below Pit organization is paramount in a 24-hour race like 'The Bol'. Tools are laid out ready to cope with any eventuality

can be won and lost by putting on the pressure, or not going for it, with hindsight, when the opportunity is presented.

This brings in the need for somebody to assume the role of team manager to organize the team to its best advantage. For instance, planning as the race progresses when to make rider changes, or if one is faster, who to keep out there for longer spells. Also to make sure the 'off' rider is ready to go in good time, and kept in touch with the race progress and what other teams are doing. A good organizer/manager can make the difference between winning and losing.

Most of the six-hour races in this country are organized so that teams have to supply their own laps scorers to record the team's progress and times and work as part of the official organization. They (a relief is required) will then score laps on official sheets from which the results will be compiled. In case you wondered, cheating is very difficult as it is done on an elapsed time basis using a digital display and marking the time shown on every lap. It is therefore largely self checking. This system is employed to save the expense of hiring several official timekeepers.

The point of mentioning this system is that inefficient lap scorers can cost you the race. Laps not recorded are lost unless each sheet is checked right through against average lap times to spot discrepancies. And there are perhaps 300 individual sheets passed up for checking so it's not possible in the time available to check every team's laps. It's a serious job and not one for the odd person you could rope in at the last moment.

Knight at Brands Hatch partnered with Richard Rose to win the Pirelli Six Hours, 750 class, on a Suzuki GSX-R

13

The tracks

I have not ridden on every track in the country, being confined by the constraints of time and money to do so. This means that my actual experience of riding the various circuits is limited mainly to the South. But I have included as many circuit maps as I can lay my hands on and committing these to memory is useful in at least knowing that the next bend is right or left, sharp or fast: it does help.

Brands Hatch

There's the Indy, a short 1.2 mile course, and the full grand prix version of over 2.6 miles. The short circuit is where the majority of club racing takes place, though the British Motor Cycle Racing Club (Bemsee) stages meetings on the full circuit three times per year. Even most of the national meetings are staged here as it's very good for spectators. It is particularly tight and demanding yet only has one really heavy braking place: Druids bend.

Being near London, Brands is a place that has made many a reputation, entries are regularly over-subscribed, everybody wants to race and win there. Meetings there are usually reported in the press and it scores high in kudos.

From the start/finish it's an uphill run for the approach to Paddock Hill bend which is one of the more difficult bends in UK circuit racing. The approach is blind in that the bend can't be seen on the approach as it's over the brow, and as you top it, the bend curves sharply right downhill, again disappearing from view.

Races are won and lost at the top of Paddock Hill, particularly on braking. A key here can be that the white line across the track towards the brow of the hill will give a place from which to judge the braking-point, depending on the speed of approach you brake at, or as late after as you dare. While the

best line going in is a wide one, holding on late towards the outside of the track before peeling off, it can leave you open to determined late-brakers sneaking up the inside.

The track drops away sharply after the apex which is in any case a little further round than it may at first seem. Trouble is, this is just as you are putting on the power to drive down the hill and the result of the bike going light over the slight hump at the apex can be to lose adhesion: the message is – treat it with caution.

The speed of the short run down the hill and then sharply up Hailwood Hill to Druids bend is of course dependent on how fast you can drive out of Paddock, but it really is one of the difficult ones to get exactly right. There's hardly time to get the bike upright and it's time to crash-brake for Druids bend, a place for the demon braker.

To the purist, there can only be one fastest line; outside, apex and outside again, however, almost anyone seems to serve here, depending on the circumstances at the time and where your opponent

Brands Hatch

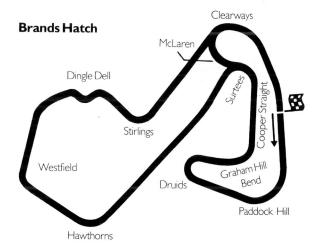

is placed. My technique of moving over to the inside of the track early while braking and going round almost on the white line serves to defend yourself against anyone sneaking up the inside and anyone trying to pass has to do so round the outside, taking the longer way and therefore travelling faster and more liable to error.

I also prefer this approach because of the better position for the sweep down, left, through Graham Hill Bend having exited Druids, there is less need to swerve from one side of the track to the other and doing just this is how many come unstuck, flicking it over too fast.

Driving steeply downhill through this corner makes it difficult yet it's where much time can be made and is the key to passing others along Cooper Straight. I find it helps to select a high gear going in and feed on as hard as possible at lower revs. Running downhill the motor will probably pull it and there's less need to change up while still banked over hard, and it will save the odd foot or two.

Peeling off left uphill into Surtees is where you leave the full circuit and go right up into Clearways. It's the place where the man who has made the fastest run along the straight will be trying to pass up the inside. The flick left/right here is the key to getting the best line into Clearways. You can drive

96

Above Coming into the broad first corner at Silverstone. The Hangar Straight at the rear of the circuit is one of the longest and fastest in the world

Left Through the chicane at Thruxton with Trevor Nation leading the pack. Races are won and lost here on late braking but it's a curving line in with the brakes still on

hard up the hill but before going over right hang on late and brake in a straight line, hard and late, before laying it right down for the acute camber on the apex of Clearways.

The key to the fastest run down the straight is power on before the apex and as hard as you can, bearing in mind the camber is falling away on the exit. This stretch is very slippery in the wet.

Going back to Surtees but using the full circuit, it's quite a strange bend with much wearing out of knee-sliders and fairings, an acute left-hander. The key is to go in particularly late so that you can power up the hill early after being right against the kerb on the apex. Going in earlier takes you up the kerb on the way out and prevents a full exit boost.

With the boost getting you a fast run up the straight you then have a drop downhill on the approach to Hawthorns' very fast right-hander. Many places are won or lost on this approach as it's difficult to judge your speed on the way in – you can't see round this one. There's another white line across the road here to help you spot the braking-point and while it's a temptation to go in so fast that you need all the engine braking to get round, it's the wrong way to do it simply because exit speed is vital here and doing so on the overrun right on the kerb rather than already driving hard will cost you yards, and places.

There's now little more than a short straight before entering the redesigned Westfield/Dingle Dell section. For 1988 Westfield became a very high-speed testing double apex right-hander sweeping steeply downhill. It takes nerve and precise positioning to get the line just right entailing using every inch of the road. Get it spot on and it's one line right through and you can gain yards on the opposition, then rocket up to the chicane that Dingle Dell has become.

There is actually a slight rise from the bottom of the hill after Westfield and before Dingle Dell. This obscures the line of sight approaching the chicane so that you need to position the bike well for what follows.

If you analyse this right/left/right, you will spot that it changes direction barely more than the width of the track. It is therefore almost possible to drive through on one line without really sweeping from side to side. It does make overtaking a push and shove job though as, like Westfield, there is really only one line through and you have to go off the ideal line to pass.

Emerging from the chicane, Stirlings' short, sharp left is next and it's one more place where the competition will try to brake up the inside as you get ready to peel off. Since this is the last bend before rejoining the short circuit at Clearways it's a vital one to take at the optimum speed while keeping the opposition at bay. And while starting from the outside of the bend is always theoretically the fastest line, a bit like Druids, it can pay to ride defensively, defending your lead from pursuers, if

indeed they are on your rear mudguard.

There's now time to get back up a couple of gears briefly running down to Clearways and it's quite different approaching it from the grand prix circuit, as opposed to the Indy track. As always, it's the adverse camber that is the problem and peeling off late can give a better drive out for the final run down to the chequered flag.

It's back then to Clearways where the approach this time is quite different. Again, a place where heavy braking up the inside can pay off as long as you can still get on to the apex to drive out fast down the straight.

The character of the grand prix circuit is different from the Indy circuit. Indy is all scratch and shoulder rubbing. Grand prix is much faster and one preferred by lovers of fast corners like myself. Having said that, I was fortunate enough to partner in the winning team in the Pirelli Six Hours race held on the short circuit in 1987, and win on the grand prix circuit in 1988.

Through the new chicane at Mallory Park. It's just a case of follow-my-leader, before the drop down to the start/finish

Cadwell Park

There are three circuits used at Cadwell Park; the full 2.2 mile Grand Prix circuit, the Club circuit and Woodlands.

Most of the club meetings take place on the Club circuit, away from the paddock. Even this can be 1.3 or 1.5 miles long, depending on which of the two possible hairpins are used.

Push-starters will welcome the downhill gradient from the grid just after Mansfield Corner. On this narrow track there is usually a skirmish at whichever of the hairpins is used. They are so short and sharp that to discuss lines is probably irrelevant, braking is so heavy that you are usually reduced to scrambling round the 180 degrees while trying to keep off the competition. There is an adverse camber on the way out though and it really pays to wait a fraction and get the bike upright before cracking open the throttle.

There's now a very steep run up into the left-hander starting at Charlies Bend, this is a particularly difficult corner – it seems to go on and on. The blind peel-off point and the adverse camber on the way out is the problem here. It precedes Park Straight and there is so much extra speed to be gained here, if you can get a fractionally faster exit from Charlies into it, that it's the place for incidents. Both the entry and exit points are most difficult to spot as the contour of the infield obscures the view so you have to judge it right by eye each time.

Park is quite steeply downhill and then up again, the place where extra power pays off. It's then into Park Corner where much outbraking takes place. You breast the rise travelling really fast and suddenly the corner comes into view and it's a crash-braking job.

Park is sharp, almost 90 degrees right and you might need second gear to get a good drive out towards Donington Curve, an awkward right-hander that curves round as you drive as hard as you dare with the bike laid over a long way and drifting all the time. It can pay to change up just before you drop it over and enter the early sharp bit, not just to reduce the chance of sliding off but to give more control while opening the throttle progressively as you drive around it.

Just as you get to the end of Donington, it tightens a shade to put you in the wrong position to drive hard downhill left into Mansfield Corner, a

Cadwell Park

sharp left-hand and right just before taking the chequered flag. Mansfield is not just a sharp bend, you are accelerating down a steep hill and it's here where the race is won or lost with last ditch braking while sneaking up the inside, or it's done to you. Finally, a quick wriggle through the following chicane and you take the flag.

On the Grand Prix track, the start/finish is on the lower straight so that you get a faster run into Charlies, and then after, going around the Club circuit, crossing the Club finish, going on past the hairpins to the Mountain, which is possibly the steepest hill I've raced up, and is preceded by a sharp left/right. The top of the mountain is such a sharp peak that a wheelie can hardly be prevented, indeed there can be a danger of losing the front wheel completely.

There's scarcely time here to get the front wheel on the ground before going through the wriggles into Hairpin Corner's very sharp, slow right. This is followed by a short bit of straight before going down into Barn Corner, the scene of much cut and thrust for the final run down to the finish.

Woodlands uses the second of the hairpins to turn from the bottom or main straight back towards the mountain and round again. This is sometimes used when mist troubles the Club circuit, it's less of a problem on the lower section of the track.

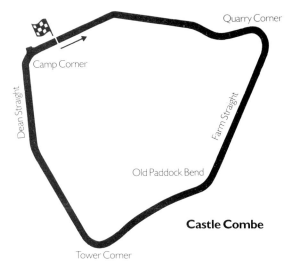

Castle Combe

Castle Combe

The 'Combe' is a forgiving and fairly flat circuit, 1.8 miles long, in that there is always plenty of grass to run out on. Yet while it's not difficult to get around quickly, it *is* difficult to get round at race winning speed. This arises from the fact there are few landmarks from which to spot the braking and peeling-off points. The local circuit specialist who has long practised the subtleties of the track really gains yards through the wide open bends.

From the start opposite the paddock, it's a flat run through the right-hand curve, whatever you are riding, towards Quarry Corner, approached through a right/left kink. This serves to put you in just the wrong place to take what is no more than a right-hander, fairly sharp, but quite acute as it seems to go on and on. But getting the entry into Farm Straight just right will help you gain several yards.

Next comes a short straight towards Old Paddock Bend and this is one that really does require a fair bit of bottle, it's so very fast, going right as quickly as you choose. No obvious spots to peel off from and you always feel that you should have taken it faster.

It's followed by what seems to be a curve left, inevitably taken flat but you again end up in what is not the classical approach to a right-hand bend. Tower Corner is a 'go for it' type bend where you tend to end up in convoy and there is only one fastest line. It's typical of the other corners, you can see round them, they are wide open and fast and lack real features.

Another fast run follows, and you'll gather that gearing is quite high at the Combe. Then on to Dean Straight, except that you have to take a right-hand curve, which is once more particularly fast and is the key to getting into Camp Corner's right-hander, the vital one before the start/finish, and where it all happens. This is where races are decided in the run to the flag.

Left **Cadwell Park's Hall Bends: Ian Wilson thunders his 1100 Suzuki into an early lead in the 1300 production race**

Right **The chairs line up for the start of a club event at Cadwell Park. This is made easy by the downhill push, then the run down to the acute hairpin and the resulting traffic jam**

Lydden

This short, sharp, twisty 1 mile track frequently offers some of the closest dicing to be found on any track I've experienced. It is so short and tortuous that it's not too difficult for a smaller, more nimble machine to beat one with twice the horsepower. A paramount factor here is braking and a smaller, lighter bike braking just a couple of yards later can pull back any advantage gained by the big machines, especially as there are precious few places where you can use the power to its full potential.

Gearing for Lydden is probably as low as it's possible to fit and you are still unlikely to use top on a big bike anyway. Getting a front row grid position can mean a big advantage, a couple of yards here is significant. The race can be won at the start as it's very difficult to pass someone who keeps to a good line and rides hard.

It seems that the road starts to drop a little just a few yards after the start and curves slightly left just as you approach the right-hander known as Pilgrims. It is difficult because as you reach the bottom of the decline, you have to be in position to drive sharp right uphill. Ideally, you'd approach it from the left-hand side of the track but somebody will try to take your line and baulk you if you haven't taken it at the optimum speed. You breast

the hill into Chessons Drift and drift you surely will on the continuing right-hander going first, up, round and then down; and it's pretty bumpy, as is most of the surface at Lydden, in fact.

On a bigger machine it's knee on the floor here with the smaller bikes sneaking up behind just starting the short, sharp run downhill into the Devils Elbow's almost vicious left-hander, where everybody tries so hard to get ahead for the run uphill to the Hairpin at North Bend.

Lydden is typically an on-off circuit: vicious acceleration between sharp corners and standing the bike on its nose on the way in. Sheer aggression

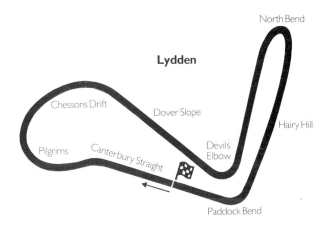

Donington Park and there are a variety of ways of tackling Redgate, neither of which seems any faster than any other. It is the place for passing and repassing – one of the most competitive corners in racing

can score here so it's wide open up the hill and then late crash-braking for the Hairpin going 180 degrees back down again and cracking it wide open again towards Paddock Bend.

Paddock is a strange sort of sharp right-hand bend. The camber is with you and you get a bit of an impression of a wall of death as you heel in late, apex, and inevitably ride up the kerb on the way out, accelerating as hard as adhesion will permit. There are just 30 yards left before the flag so Paddock is the place where lots of passing up the inside takes place and the guy on the outside frequently ends up getting run right up the kerb.

Mallory Park

This is another really tight and demanding circuit, 1.35 miles long and a bit like a cross between Brands' short track and Lydden. It was modified for the 1987 season and a chicane added before the run downhill to Devils Elbow to reduce speed, through what was obviously thought to be a dangerous section.

The real feature of the circuit is Gerrards bend. From the start/finish on Kirkby Straight there's just enough room to sort out the pack a little before tackling the long, fast 180-degree sweeper, laid over as far as you're likely to at that speed. It's a place where getting the entry right makes so much difference and also one where you tend to go in on the overrun, backing the throttle, before pulling it back on gradually as you go round and if you are right on speed and line it is taken in one, accelerating all the way.

Silverstone

There are two versions of this famous circuit, that has hosted the British Grand Prix and Clubman's Championship final. It's reckoned to be one of the safer tracks around with lots of run-off areas and is very wide and fast on nearly all of the corners. It provides the ultimate opportunities for slipstreaming and overtaking going into corners.

There aren't many bike meetings at Silverstone though the Club, 1.6 mile, short circuit does have the Motor Cycling Club meeting every year with its half-hour trials and scratch races and it is where I made my own debut back in 1958. I even held the lap record there on a Royal Enfield Meteor for a couple of years.

This might well be described as the ideal beginners' course. Its four corners are all quite straightforward and with varying degrees of right-hander, except for Maggotts' left-hand curve which you can take flat if you judge it well on the way in.

From the wide open spaces of the grid that can take up to 50 machines, it's a rush into Copse Corner and the only concern is a slightly adverse camber just falling away as you try to crack on everything you can find on the exit. The chequered kerbs are used by the adventurous though not recommended when it's wet. There are braking marker-boards on the approach to all the corners to help you save vital yards on the way in.

Maggotts Curve is a real blinder and quick men will lay an 1100 over and drive through the left-hander and down towards Becketts, which is a hairpin on the short circuit and leads out on to the Grand Prix track.

It's here that determined braking can pay off and since the fastest run through Maggotts will put you on the inside of the track anyway, it tends to be something of a scramble to get round but it is so wide open it's perhaps no bad thing to be on the inside as the opposition always try to sneak through here and it's the best way to defend your position. You can see all combinations of line on this one whatever the purist line should really be, almost everyone seems as fast as the next person.

The essence, however, is trying to get the best possible exit speed for the very long straight that follows which is something like two-thirds of a mile. It is slightly uphill and the place to prove that your bike is half a mile per hour faster than your opponent's.

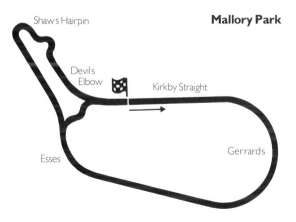

Mallory Park

Shaw's Hairpin

Devils Elbow

Kirkby Straight

Esses

Gerrards

Silverstone

On a very wet grid at Silverstone. Wet tyres will be fitted that give an incredible amount of grip compared to normal treaded, road tyres

The approach to Woodcote Corner is frequently the race decider as so many bikes these days have similar performances. It's the big braking job here before the flag just around the corner where it's all decided. Particularly when you compete in the High-Speed Trials, you have the chance to aim at cutting the distance down each time by the marker-boards provided. Then after a long run down the straight in a faster bike's slipstream, you can pull out knowing just how late you can possibly leave it to sneak the race, I mean, trial. If you do the trial, you'll find out what I'm talking about.

On the Grand Prix circuit, which is over 2.9 miles, Becketts is the slowest corner on the track, quite sharp right that goes a little further round than you anticipate, to put you in the wrong place for the swerve left into the long Hangar Straight. The quick change of direction can be a hazard in itself.

If you managed to keep over to the right-hand side of the track driving into Chapel's gentle left it's no problem but you are travelling fast through there and if you have to ease the throttle on the way out through running wide, you'll lose yards to the competition.

Braking is the key to Stowe Corner's fast right. It really is very quick and in the desperation of

dicing within a pack, rushing up the inside and scrambling round seems to be the order of the day just to sneak a place.

Club Corner is just a few hundred yards' dash away and you may go up and down a gear in the process. Club is difficult to gauge because the road falls away a little and for a moment you can lose sight of it as there's just a slight rise on the apex. Until you get really brave you will always feel that you didn't go through fast enough as there always seems to be a yard or two to spare on the way out. It's very quick and the really fast men make yards here and use all the road way out to the kerb on the exit. I've seen Kenny Roberts deliberately ride several feet over the, admittedly low, kerb every lap and use the tarmac outside it. He'd obviously meticulously checked out just how much track there really was at that point and found some that few others except Randy Mamola used.

The following Abbey Curve left-hander is as fast as you dare. Concise positioning and nerve will get you through on almost anything without knocking it back. It's got ripples on the apex and you are laid over quite enough even for the inveterate scratchers to enjoy it. It is, however, a vitally important corner because it's not too far to the flag.

Getting a wheel in front on the drive into Woodcote can mean win or lose, but Woodcote itself is particularly fast and wide open so that somebody will always go for it and try to drive on the inside or outside of you if you leave any chance.

And so to the chequered flag on what is the fastest circuit on the mainland.

Snetterton

This circuit is 1.9 miles long and pretty flat, but is nevertheless interesting, taking in as it does, fast and slow corners and a long straight to let the big bikes have their head.

The start is slightly uphill and as long as push-starting is employed it can pose a problem shoving a big Jap multi fast enough to make a bump start. Even on a clutch start, though, the 150-odd yards before Riches' right-hander is sufficient to sort the pack out a little.

Riches is a quick bend and with what looks like at first sight to be a double apex but is taken in one sweep. Braking is key here and there are marker-boards to assist, also some marks on the track due to resurfacing, until they too get resurfaced. It's a place for overtaking moves as opponents try to sneak up the inside. It's also the place to get the power on early and the surface is smooth but very slippery in the wet.

Since the following Sear Corner is a sharp right-hander and a spot for late brakers, those who got a quick exit from Riches will be placed to overtake going into the 90-degree corner. It seems to be a place for plenty of action where late-late-brakers use plenty of tarmac to run out of road or overdo it altogether, or enthusiastic power on early men lose the back end trying to get the fastest run into the long straight. Again there's plenty of concrete to spare, typical of most of the Snetterton bends.

The Revett Straight is over half a mile long and the place for slipstreaming faster machines if you can get tucked in coming out of Sear. What really makes it is the heavy braking at the end into The Esses; long left and short right. The place for both the brave men and calculated late-brakers. Those who miscalculate will be glad of the long run-on area if they get it wrong, and most regain the track by going down it and rejoin just before the Bailey Bridge.

Braking while still laid over wins the day on Esses One, even though the heavy bit is done between the

Snetterton

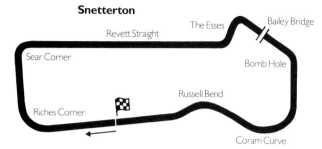

200- and 100-yard marker-boards. It is here where there is always much jockeying for advantage as everybody tries for the lead going into Esses Two, otherwise known as the Hairpin.

There is seldom the chance to use what is probably the fastest line through this section, sweeping left on braking right to the outside of the track before peeling off into the tight right and getting a better run towards the Bomb Hole. If somebody is that close, and they always seem to be, it gives them the chance to slip up the inside and get a wheel in front at the apex of the Hairpin. Conversely, you can try it yourself.

Just 30-odd yards now in which to accelerate under the Bridge over which you drove on the way into the paddock. The dip and right-hander in front of the stand is referred to as the Bomb Hole and you can benefit from using every inch of the road on the outside before peeling off into it and driving hard out.

Coram Curve which follows next is the real feature of Snetterton in that the sweeping right-hander goes on long enough for plenty of overtaking moves on the way in, out and through and it's where fairings and knees contact the ground at speed. On a fast machine, having backed it off on the entry you accelerate all the way around it perhaps enough to grab the advantage as you run slightly downhill into Russell Bend, actually a left/right combination.

Braver types can make a lot of time through here and it's where races to the start/finish are won and lost. It's the place where hanging back a little on the last lap when chasing hard, going for the 'balls out' run through and getting a tow up your opponent's slipstream on the drive out, can get you across the line with a wheel in front.

Snetterton is also one of the few circuits suited to endurance racing and in the 1987 season there were two Pirelli Six Hours Championship rounds plus the Bantam Racing Club's Six Hours.

Thruxton

Thruxton, a 2.4 mile course, offers a particularly fast, long curve that is really its prime feature and an almost unique challenge.

From the start/finish on Pit Straight, Allard Corner comes up very fast right and the track here seems very wide and open. Just knocking the throttle back on the 100-yard sign seems to do the trick well enough. What it also does is to put you on the outside of the track faced with a left curve and there's little else but to drive round it hugging the curve, because next is the short, sharp Campbell-Cobb-Segrave section; sharp right/left/right, a real scratcher's paradise throwing the bike on its side each time.

The approach is slightly complicated by the fact that it is both slightly downhill and is still curving left. You therefore need to be on the left of the track to get a good entry into Campbell's right, then on to position for the sweep left through Cobb and be well placed for the fastest drive 'out into the country' through Segrave, which is fast right – if you can get the attack right.

After the scratcher's section it's time for the fast, sweeping Kimpton 'ess' and it's going for it in fourth or fifth, depending what's under you. It's bumpy and testing and precedes Village Curve which just curves right and seemingly on over the horizon. You always appear to be in the wrong position going in, yet somehow it never quite matters.

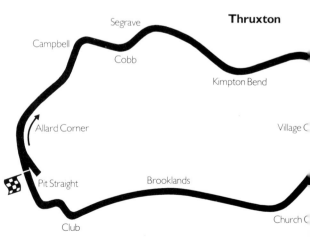

Village must be one of the longest curves in the business and it's a place for the brave to get stuck in and wind it up with their right knee on the floor. It's around and around going right and then slightly downhill to Church Corner, more of an almost flat out in fourth or fifth job as hard as you dare to get the fastest run up the long, curving hill named Brooklands.

The approach to Club corner is a real tester and where sneaky braking pays off. It's tricky because the road curves right while you are attempting a late braking job, and getting into the chicane first just before the start/finish means races won and lost. This really is one to get right. There are just 40–50 yards now to the flag to try and get back in front.

Lydden, Kent is an interesting circuit with demanding, sharp inclines

Appendix 1: Circuits

Aberdare Park

Situated 24 miles north of Cardiff.

Aberaman MCC
P. G. Davies
42 King Street
Cwmdare, Aberdare
Mid Glamorgan

Aintree

Situated off M57 north of Liverpool.

Aintree MCRC
E. J. Richards
7 Sandfield Close
West Derby
Liverpool L12 2AD

Brands Hatch

Brands Hatch Leisure Ltd
Fawkham
Dartford
Kent DA3 8NG
Tel: 0474 872331

Situated on the A20, 20 miles south-east of London
between Swanley and Wrotham.

BMCRC
T. Mount
Brands Hatch Circuit
Fawkham
Dartford
Kent DA3 8NG
Tel: 0474 872331

Kent Racing Combine
J. Ward
'Ivydene', 15 Pilgrims Road,
North Halling
nr Rochester
Kent

Triumph Owners Club
S. Mellish
4 Douglas Avenue
Harold Wood
Romford
Essex RM3 0UT
Tel: 04023 42684

Vintage MCC
Mrs K. Lowe
c/o 42 Haddon Crescent
Chilwell
Notts. NG9 5JT
Tel: 0602 259310

Cadwell Park

Brands Hatch Leisure Ltd
Cadwell Park
nr Louth
Lincs. LN11 9SE
Tel: 0507 84248

Situated on the A153 between Horncastle and Louth.

Auto 66 Club
P. Hillaby
New Road
Nafferton
Driffield
N. Humberside YO25 0JP
Tel: 0377 44727

Bantam Racing Club
Mrs J. Walpole
6 Kipton Close,
Rothwell
Northants NN14 2DR
Tel: 0536 710674

Cheshire MCRRC
L. Bibby
6 Berwick Avenue
Eastham
Merseyside L62 8EB
Tel: 051 327 2549

Classic RMC
Mrs B. Miller
65 Hillmead
Gossops Green
Crawley
Sussex RH11 8RP

Clubmans Racing Club
J. Parker
172 Tower Road
Ware
Herts. SG12 7LL
Tel: 0920 5559

Derby Phoenix MCC
B. J. Charles
21 Corporation Road
Ilkeston
Derbyshire

Formula 5 MCRC (Barnsley) Ltd
A. Glover
11 Parma Rise
Darfield
Barnsley S73 9PR
Tel: 0226 754 278

Louth & DMC
K. Briggs
Old Manor House
Cadwell Park
nr Louth
Lincs. LN11 9SE
Tel: 0507 84248

Midland MCRC
Miss J. Andrews
230 Holt Road
Wrexham
Clwyd LL13 7EE
Tel: 0978 290167

New Era MCC
Mrs J. Maslin
172 Tower Road
Ware
Herts. SG12 7LL
Tel: 0920 5559

Newmarket MCC
J. Coates
31 Rowley Drive
Newmarket
Suffolk CB8 0JL
Tel: 0638 662698

Pegasus MCC
K. Awcock
39 Belvoir Gardens
Great Gonerby
Grantham
Lincs.

Retford & DMCC
Mrs K. Swannack
26 Holme Hall Avenue
Bottesford
Scunthorpe
S. Humberside DN16 3PZ

Skegness & DMCC
Mrs J. Bingham
Old River Bank
Wainfleet
Skegness
Lincs. PE24 4ND
Tel: 057 482 205

Velocette Owners Club
B. Clarke
57 Jireh Court
Ferrymount Road
Haywards Heath
Surrey RH16 1BH

Vincent Owners Club
Mrs M. Alexander
44 Mancetter Road
Atherstone
War. CV9 1NZ

Vintage MCC
Mrs K. Lowe
c/o 42 Haddon Crescent
Chilwell
Notts. NG9 5JT
Tel: 0602 259310

Carnaby

Situated $1\frac{1}{2}$ miles west of Bridlington, N. Humberside.

Auto 66 Club
P. Hillaby
New Road
Nafferton
Driffield
N. Humberside YO25 0JP
Tel: 0377 44727

Castle Combe

Castle Combe Circuit
Mr H. Strawford
Westway Farm
Upper Castle Combe
nr Chippenham
Wilts.
Tel: 0249 782395

Situated 5 miles north-west of Chippenham on B4039.

North Glos. MCC
W. B. Underwood
61 Bispham Road
London NW1 7HB

Colerne

Situated 8 miles west-south-west of Chippenham, Wilts.

North Glos. MCC
W. B. Underwood
61 Bispham Road
London NW1 7HB

Darley Moor

Situated Ashbourne-Uttoxeter main road.

Darley Moor MCRRC
E. Nelson
Anvil House
Derby Road
Old Tupton
Chesterfield
Derbyshire S42 6LA

Donington Park

Donington Park Racing Ltd
Castle Donington
Derby DE7 5RP
Tel: 0332 810048

Situated 8 miles south-east of Derby.

ACU
Miller House
Corporation Street
Rugby
War. CV21 2DN
Tel: 0788 540519

Classic RMC
Mrs B. Miller
65 Hillmead
Gossops Green
Crawley
Sussex RH11 8RP

Clubmans Racing Club
J. Parker
172 Tower Road
Ware
Herts. SG12 7LL
Tel: 0920 5559

Donington 100 RC Ltd
Mrs V. E. Smith
21 Tamworth Street
Duffield
Derby DE6 4ER

Pathfinders & Derby MCC
B. Tuxford
15 Westhall Road
Mickleover
Derby DE3 5PA
Tel: 0332 516861

Retford & DMCC
Mrs K. Swannack
26 Holme Hall Avenue
Bottesford
Scunthorpe
S. Humberside DN16 3PZ

Vintage MCC
Mrs K. Lowe
c/o 42 Haddon Crescent
Chilwell
Notts. NG9 5JT
Tel: 0602 259310

Elvington Airfield

RAF Elvington, nr York.

Situated 4 miles south-east of York.

Auto 66 Club
P. Hillaby
New Road
Nafferton
Driffield
N. Humberside YO25 0JP
Tel: 0377 44727

NSA
Mrs J. Sykes
10 Compton Street
Clifton
Yorks. YO3 6LE

Keevil Airfield

New Keevil Village, Wilts.

Situated 5 miles east of Trowbridge.

North Glos. MCC
W. B. Underwood
61 Bispham Road
London NW1 7HB

Knockhill Racing Circuit

Fife, KY12 9XX, Scotland.

Situated 5 miles north of Dunfermline on the A823. Take Junction 4 from the M90 and signposted thereafter.

Contact Derek Butcher: circuit no. 0383 723337, home no. 0592 891 211.

Knockhill MCRC
Mrs B. Chapman
Bankier
Backmuir
nr Dunfermline
Fife Y12 8QR
Tel: 0383 721042

Long Marston

Situated A46 near Stratford-upon-Avon.

NDRA
M. Rumbold
61 Chedworth Close
Church Hill
Redditch
Worcs. B98 8QT

Lydden

William Mark Holdings Ltd
Mr W. Chesson
71 West Street
Sittingbourne
Kent NE10 1AN

Situated A2, 6 miles north of Dover.

Astra MCC/E. Grinstead & DMCC/Double Five (Kent) MCC
Miss B. J. Harris
71 West Street
Sittingbourne
Kent NE10 1AN
Tel: 0795 71978/72926

Bantam Racing Club
Mrs J. Walpole
6 Kipton Close
Rothwell
Northants NN14 2DR
Tel: 0536 710674

Triumph Owners Club
S. Mellish
4 Douglas Avenue
Harold Wood
Romford
Essex RM3 0UT
Tel: 04023 42684

Mallory Park

Mrs E. Overend
Mallory Park
Kirkby Mallory
nr Hinckley
Leics.
Tel: 0455 42931

Situated off the A47 and A447, between Hinckley and Leicester.

Auto 66 Club
P. Hillaby
New Road
Nafferton
Driffield
N. Humberside YO25 0JP
Tel: 0377 44727

Classic RMC
Mrs B. Miller
65 Hillmead
Gossops Green
Crawley
Sussex RH11 8RP

Clubmans Racing Club
J. Parker
172 Tower Road
Ware
Herts. SG12 7LL
Tel: 0920 5559

Derby Phoenix MCC
B. J. Charles
21 Corporation Road
Ilkeston
Derbyshire

EMRA
M. Jessup
53 Coombe Drive
Binley Woods
Coventry CV3 2QU

Pegasus MCC
K. Awcock
39 Belvoir Gardens
Great Gonerby
Grantham
Lincs.

Retford & DMCC
Mrs K. Swannack
26 Holme Hall Avenue
Bottesford
Scunthorpe
S. Humberside DN16 3PZ

Vintage MCC
Mrs K. Lowe
c/o 42 Haddon Crescent
Chilwell
Notts. NG9 5JT
Tel: 0602 259310

Oulton Park

Cheshire Car Circuit Ltd
Little Budworth
Tarporley
Cheshire CW6 9BW
Tel: 082 921 301/302

Situated off A54 near Tarporley in Cheshire.

Cheshire ACU
N. Howell
10 Hatchmere Road
Great Boughton
Chester
Tel: 0244 318468

Cheshire MCRRC
L. Bibby
6 Berwick Avenue
Eastham
Merseyside L62 8EB
Tel: 051 327 2549

Nantwich & DMCC
K. Beckett
8 Forge Fields
Wheelock
Sandbach
Cheshire CW11 0QN

Wirral 100 MC
Mrs M. Dewsnap
9 Westmoreland Road
Wallasey
Merseyside L45 1HU

Ouston

Albemarle Barracks
Ouston
Northumberland

North East MCRC
M. Barkess
20 Glenesk Road
Sunderland
Tyne & Wear SR2 9BN

Pembrey

Nr Llanelli
Dyfed
South Wales

Aberaman MCC
P. G. Davies
42 King Street
Cwmdare
Aberdare
Mid Glamorgan
Tel: 0685 876208

Classic RMC
Mrs B. Miller
65 Hillmead
Gossops Green
Crawley
Sussex RH11 8RP

Midland MCRC
Miss J. Andrews
230 Holt Road
Wrexham
Clwyd LL13 7EE
Tel: 0978 290167

Port Talbot MCRC
Mrs S. Lawrence
80 Tyn-y-Twr
Baglan
Port Talbot
W. Glamorgan

Santa Pod

Santa Pod Promotions Ltd
98 Martins Road
Shortlands
Bromley
Kent
Tel: 01 290 0090

BDRA
Mrs Y. Tramm
Bakerfield
29 West Drive
Caldecote
Cambs. CB3 7NY
Tel: 0954 210028

Scarborough

Olivers Mount
Scarborough

Scarborough RC
P. Hillaby
New Road
Nafferton
Driffield
N. Humberside YO25 0JP
Tel: 0377 44727

Silverstone

Silverstone Circuit
Silverstone
nr Towcester
Northants NN12 8TN
Tel: 0327 857271

Situated between Towcester and Brackley on A43.

ACU
Miller House
Corporation Street
Rugby
War. CV21 2DN
Tel: 0788 540519

The Motor Cycling Club
H. Tucker-Peake
Upperstone Croft
nr Buckingham MK15 4JA

Morgan Three Wheeler Club
L. Weeks
101 Shawhurst Lane
Hollywood
Birmingham B47 5JP

Snetterton

Snetterton Circuit
Snetterton
Norwich
Norfolk NR16 2JU
Tel: 095387 303/304

Situated on A11 London to Norwich Road, between Thetford and Attleborough.

Bantam Racing Club
Mrs J. Walpole
6 Kipton Close
Rothwell
Northants NN14 2DR
Tel: 0536 710674

BMCRC
T. Mount
Brands Hatch Circuit
Fawkham
Dartford
Kent DA3 8NG

Classic RMC
Mrs B. Miller
65 Hillmead
Gossops Green
Crawley
Sussex RH11 8RP

Clubmans Racing Club
J. Parker
172 Tower Road
Ware
Herts SG12 7LL
Tel: 0920 5559

Formula 5 MCRC
A. Glover
11 Parma Rise
Darfield
Barnsley
S. Yorks. S73 9PR
Tel: 0226 754278

Midland MCRC
Miss J. Andrews
230 Holt Road
Wrexham
Clwyd LL13 7EE
Tel: 0978 290167

Newmarket MCC
J. Coates
31 Rowley Drive
Newmarket
Suffolk CB8 0JL
Tel: 0638 662698

Snetterton Combine
C. Armes
33 Falcon Road East
Norwich
Norfolk NR7 8XZ
Tel: 0603 45749

Vintage MCC Ltd
Mrs K. Lowe
c/o 42 Haddon Crescent
Chilwell
Notts. NG9 5JT
Tel: 0602 259310

Three Sisters Circuit

Nr Ashton in Makerfield, Lancs.

Bolton MCC
P. Manley
The Dell
Delph Brook Way
Egerton
Bolton
Lancs. BL7 9SH

North Western Centre ACU
M. E. Simpson
2 Marsden Grove
Brierfield
Nelson
Lancs.
Tel: 0282 694140

Preston & DMCC
W. Jackson
3 Greystoke Close
Bamber Bridge
Preston PR5 6YS

Shaw & DMCC
P. Johnson
24 Scarr Lane
Shaw
Oldham
Lancs. OL2 8HQ
Tel: 0706 843129

Vintage MCC
Mrs K. Lowe
c/o 42 Haddon Crescent
Chilwell
Notts NG9 5JT
Tel: 0602 259310

Thruxton

BARC (Thruxton) Ltd
Thruxton Circuit
Andover
Hants.
Tel: 026477 2607/2696

Situated 2 miles outside Andover on Hants/Wilts.
border, A303 Amesbury.

Clubmans Racing Club
J. Parker
172 Tower Road
Ware
Herts. SG12 7LL
Tel: 0920 5559

Southampton & DMC
L. Harfield
Kenton
Bridge Road
Burlesdon
Southampton

West Raynham

Situated 5 miles south-west of Fakenham, Norfolk.

Bantam Racing Club
Mrs J. Walpole
6 Kipton Close
Rothwell
Northants. NN14 2DR
Tel: 0536 710674

Newmarket MCC
J. Coates
31 Rowley Drive
Newmarket
Suffolk
CB8 0JL
Tel: 0638 662698

Isle of Man

Billown

Nr Castletown.

Southern 100 MC
G. C. Goddard
24 Victoria Road
Castletown
IOM
Tel: 0624 822411

Jurby South and Jurby Airfield

Situated 7 miles west of Ramsey, 3 miles north of
Ballaugh.

Andreas Racing Association
E. N. Bowers
4 Finch Road
Douglas
IOM

TT Mountain

ACU
Miller House
Corporation Street
Rugby
War. CV21 2DN
Tel: 0788 540519

Manx MCC
W. L. Bennett
Fourth Floor
Viking House
Nelson Street
Douglas
IOM
Tel: 0624 27434

*Address for licence applications and all matters relating
to road racing:*

The Auto Cycle Union
Road Racing Dept
Miller House
Corporation Street
Rugby
War. CV21 2DN
Tel: 0788 70332

Appendix 2: Regulations

These various regulations, extracted from the 1988 Auto Cycle Union Handbook, govern the machine specifications for the machines, what you can and cannot do to them. Please consult the most recent edition of this handbook for any amendments.

There are in fact two classes of Production races, ACU Clubman's Formula Specification and ACU TT Production Machine Championship. Newcomers to the game will only be concerned with the former, applying as they do to meetings at club status. As the name implies, the latter are for National Championship events and the Isle of Man TT races. Club racing regulations are somewhat looser regarding how much preparation can be carried out, examples of which are that air filters may be removed and the cylinder-head faces machined to increase compression ratios. The TT regulations are strict in requiring no changes to the machine apart from those in the interests of safety.

The general regulations covering all race machines are reproduced to give guidance to those who are preparing open-class racing machines. As well as the rules covering any of the particular classes of machine, all bikes have to conform to those.

ACU Clubman's Formula Specification

Specification of a Sports Motorcycle for all production machine races held under an ACU permit.

1 Machines must be complete, fully equipped motorcycles of a model/marque to UK specifications, as originally assembled at the factory of a recognized manufacturer, for road use in a minimum quantity of 100.

The only permitted alterations are detailed in 2, 3 and 5 below.

2(a) Handlebars – any shape of handlebar is permitted provided that it is fitted in the original mounting position only.

(b) Footrests and foot controls – proprietary rearsets are acceptable but must comply with Rule 5 below and ACU Standing Regulations.

(c) Gearing – the sprockets may be changed. The final drive chain specification must remain standard in respect of width and pitch.

(d) Friction linings, disc pads and brake hoses may be changed.

(e) Compression springs and damping may be changed, but the original mountings must be used.

(f) Exhaust systems – no modification is permitted.

(g) Rebores – to allow for wear, rebores will be permitted, but only to the maximum of the manufacturer's recommended rebore sizes.

(h) Air filter elements may be removed. Air box assemblies must not be modified.

(i) The addition of the following is permitted – security bolts and screws, steering dampers, fork braces, engine protection bars (see Rule 5).

(j) Carburettors – no modification other than a change of jet size is permitted.

(k) Compression ratio – cylinder head joint faces may be machined – the external appearance of the engine must remain unaltered. Where originally specified, a solid head gasket must be retained.

(l) Side stand mounting lugs may be removed.

(m) Throttle controls – must be self-closing as Standing Regulation 11.

3 The following alterations MUST be made.

(a) Licence holders, club badges (except transfers), centre and prop-stands, luggage carriers, mirrors and rear registration plate (but NOT tail light) must be removed. Indicators may be retained at the discretion of the rider but, if retained, the glasses must be taped.

(b) Where breather pipes are fitted they must discharge via existing outlets into a catch tank as per ACU Standing Regulation No. 14.

(c) Head lamp and rear light glasses must be adequately taped to prevent splintering.

(d) Stop lamps must be disconnected and their glasses taped.

(e) Tyres – RACING TYRES or H and V rated road tyres

MUST be used. It is NOT permissible to alter any part of the machine to accommodate wider tyres. Slick tyres are not permitted. The depth of the tyre tread must be at least 2.5 mm.

4 All electrical equipment fitted must be in working order except the stop lamp which MUST be disconnected.

5 No addition or alteration by machining, welding, brazing, silver soldering or bonding may be carried out externally to any part of the machine.

ACU TT Production Machine Championship Regulations

1 Machine eligibility
(a) Machines must be available in the UK on 1 June 1988 in a quantity of not less than 100 units. No machine which is 5 years old or more is eligible to compete. It is the manufacturer's responsibility to prove availability of machines and on request provide the scrutineer with specification details in English.

2 Machine specification
(a) Machines must be raced as supplied by a manufacturer in road legal condition, with all electrics in working order. No tuning or fettling of any sort is permitted except where specified in these regulations, the criterion for which will be safety.

No modification is permitted to exhaust systems other than the fitting of rubbing strips.

Air filters may not be removed, air box assemblies must not be modified.

Standard handlebars must be retained.

Carburettors – no modification other than a change of jet size within 10% is permitted.

(b) For classification purposes a factor of 2 to 1 will be used in determining the cc of turbocharged machines.

3 Permitted modifications
(a) The following items must be removed: Licence holders, club badges (except transfers), centre stands, stop light/rear light bulbs, indicator bulbs, stalk mirrors, rear registration plate or any item of non-original equipment.

(b) The following items may be removed: stub mirrors, side stands and mounting brackets or lugs for side stands, dualseat conversion where supplied as original equipment, indicators, rear brake light switches.

(c) Where breather pipes are fitted they must discharge via existing outlets into a catch tank, in accordance with the Sporting Code.

(d) All lights, stop and rear light assemblies must not be removed but all lens covers and mirrors must be taped to reduce splintering.

(e) H or V rated tyres or the radial equivalent must be used. Only those tyres on general sale to the public as road legal tyres will be permitted. The use of 'specials', although road legal, is strictly forbidden. 'Suspect' tyres will be retained for comparison with a tyre purchased from a retailer and any contravention of the rule may lead to disqualification of the rider. The depth of the tyre tread must be at least 2.5 mm.

Alterations to machines to accommodate oversize tyres are not permitted.

(f) Three number plates must be affixed to the machine unless otherwise stated in the Supplementary Regulations. Number plates must conform to Standing Regulation No. 22.

(g) A steering damper may be fitted but this must be done in a workmanlike manner and be approved by the chief scrutineer. No part of the machine may be removed or modified in any way to accommodate the damper or its brackets. The only part of the machine which may be modified to accommodate the steering damper is the lock stops which must be altered to reduce the lock of the machine up to the minimum as specified in the FIM Code. Under no circumstances will a machine be accepted where the steering damper and the point at which the damper is anchored to the chassis acts as the lock stop.

4 Optional equipment
The following optional equipment may be used:

(a) Brake friction linings, disc pads, brake hoses and couplings may be changed in the interests of safety.

(b) Footrests, foot controls and rear master cylinders may be changed to accommodate left or right gear/brake changes providing this does not advantage the ground clearance of the machine. Proprietary rearsets are acceptable. The minimum of parts may be changed or removed to accomplish the above but the assembly must be no less than 95% of the weight of the original including the gear shift spindle.

(c) Rebores up to a maximum of 1 mm or manufacturer's recommended oversize (whichever is the lesser) are permitted.

(d) Tyre security – screws and bolts are permitted.

(e) Chains – the original pitch of the chain must be retained but proprietary brands of chain may be fitted. Chain guards, where fitted, must remain in the original position.

(f) Gearing – the sprockets may be changed. The final drive chain specification must remain standard in respect of pitch.

(g) Machines may be altered within the limits provided by the manufacturer on the standard machine i.e. chain tensioning, damper adjustment front and rear, fork height option parts may not be fitted. However, fork oils, type and quantity, plugs, lubricant and fuel, tyre pressure and content inner tubes (if fitted), wheel balance weights and tubeless valves (if fitted) may be changed.

(*h*) No addition or alteration may be made to the machine by machining, welding, brazing, soldering or bonding with the exception of the changing of the foot controls, mounting of number plates, steering dampers and affixing of oil or petrol catch tanks.

(*j*) Exhaust rubbing strips are permitted.

(*k*) In the case of a two-stroke machine; if a separate oiling system is fitted as standard, it must be connected and functioning as the manufacturer intended.

(*l*) The chief scrutineer will have the right to reject the optional equipment specified in these regulations if he feels that it is not constructed in the spirit of these regulations.

Any item not specifically mentioned in these regulations must remain to the manufacturer's original specifications.

Road Racing

The National Sporting Code of the ACU and the Standing Regulations together with the Supplementary Regulations and any final instructions shall apply to all Road Races.

1 **Eligibility** For NATIONAL COMPETITIONS, Entrants, Drivers and Passengers must hold a current Competition Licence for International or National Road Race Events issued by the ACU, the Scottish ACU, or the MCU of Ireland.

For all competitions of BELOW NATIONAL STATUS, a current Competition Licence of the appropriate grade is required. Details of eligibility will be found in the Supplementary Regulations of the Event.

2 **Specifications of motorcycles** Motorcycles must comply with the following requirements.

3 **Brakes** Motorcycles in Category A1 and A2 (Solos) must be equipped with one efficient brake, operating on each wheel, and operated independently.

Motorcycles in Category B1 and B2 (Three-Wheelers) must be equipped with at least two brakes, operating independently on at least two of the road wheels, each giving complete control from the riding position.

All vehicles in group B2 must have the following braking system.

(*a*) One main system with at least two circuits operating separately. One of the circuits must work upon at least 2 of the 3 wheels.

(*b*) An emergency system operated by the handlebar lever with a simple circuit operated on the front or rear wheel of the motorcycle.

4 **Size of wheel rims and tyres** For solo motorcycles, the wheel rims must be at least 400 mm (16 in.) in diameter. No alteration shall be permitted to the spokes or rims of alloy wheels. Tyres must have the following dimensions:

Classes	Minimum Rim		Minimum Tyre Width
	Rim Marking	Inside Width mm	mm
Front Wheels	Marking	mm	mm
51 cc to 125 cc	1.50/WM0	38	50
126 cc to 250 cc	1.50/WM0	38	63
251 cc to 350 cc	1.60/WM1	40.5	70
351 cc to 500 cc	1.85/WM1	47	75
501 cc to 1300 cc	2.15/WM2	55	83
Rear Wheels	Marking	mm	mm
51 cc to 125 cc	1.50/WM0	38	50
126 cc to 250 cc	1.50/WM1	40.5	70
251 cc to 350 cc	1.85/WM1	47	83
351 cc to 500 cc	2.15/WM2	55	100
501 cc to 1300 cc	2.15/WM3	55	110

NOTE: Minimum tyre widths to be considered maximum for vintage machines.

(a) *Tyres for Solos*
For all National meetings the use of slick tyres is permitted. For meetings below National Restricted status, only tyres having a moulded tread pattern are permitted, hand cut slicks are not permitted. The minimum tread depth must be 2.5 mm unless otherwise stated in Championship Conditions.

(b) *Tyres for Sidecars and Three-Wheelers*
For all meetings, the use of slick tyres is permitted. For sidecars and three-wheelers (Categories B1, B2 and B3), the wheel rims shall be at least 254 mm in diameter and 64 mm in width. The diameter of the tyre must be at least 400 mm and the width 100 mm, maximum front tyre width 220 mm.

(c) *Tubeless Tyres (Solos and Sidecars)*
If a tyre is to be run tubeless it is recommended that the internal rim dimensions are approved by the manufacturer of the tyres being used. Tyre/rim relationship for tubeless application is very critical.

(d) *Slick Tyres*
The surface of a slick tyre must contain three or more hollows at 120-degree intervals or less, indicating the limit of wear on the centre and shoulder areas of the tyre. When at least two of these indicator hollows become worn on different parts of the periphery, the tyre must no longer be used. Whenever races are held in which slick tyres are being used, a warming up lap or laps may be included at the discretion of the Clerk of the Course.

5 **Clutch and brake levers** Clutch and brake levers must be ball ended, the diameter of the ball being not less than

19 mm and either an integral part of the lever, or a permanent fixture.

6 Mudguards Mudguards are not compulsory. If fitted, the following rules will apply:

They must project laterally beyond the tyre on each side. The rear mudguard must cover at least 120 degrees of the circumference of the rear wheel, and the angle contained by a line drawn from the rear end of the rear mudguard to the centre of the rear road wheel and a line drawn horizontally through the centre of the road wheel must not exceed 20 degrees.

The front mudguard must cover not less than 100 degrees of the circumference of the front road wheel. The angle contained by a line drawn from the rear end of the front mudguard to the centre of the front road wheel and a line drawn horizontally through the centre of that road wheel must not exceed 20 degrees. Similarly, the angle contained by a line drawn from the front end of the front mudguard to the centre of the front road wheel and a line drawn horizontally through the centre of that road wheel must not be less than 45 degrees nor more than 60 degrees.

7 Primary drive An adequate guard must be fitted to prevent the drive being accidentally touched at any part of the run not in contact with the sprockets.

8 Exhaust pipes The end of the exhaust pipe or pipes must not project beyond any part of the vehicle or its bodywork. Exhaust gases must not be discharged so as to raise dust or foul the tyres or brakes, or inconvenience a following driver. Any provision for the discharge of waste or surplus oil must be so made that it does not inconvenience a following driver. The end of the exhaust pipe for a minimum distance of 30 mm must be horizontal and parallel (within a ± 10 degree tolerance) to the fore and aft centre line of the machine. It must not extend beyond a line drawn at a vertical tangent to the rear edge of the motorcycle rear tyre.

For sidecars the exhaust pipes must not extend beyond the limits of the sidecar on the sidecar side and must not extend more than 330 mm from the centre of the machine on the opposite side unless contained within the streamlining.

9 Control of exhaust noise The Clerk of the Course may exclude any machine which exceeds the maximum permitted level.

The permitted noise level shall be 110 dBA with a plus 5 dBA tolerance for four-stroke machines only. The method and conditions for the measurement of noise emitted by a motorcycle shall be the official FIM test as follows:

The microphone shall be placed 0.5 m from each exhaust pipe outlet at an angle of 45 degrees from the rear end of the centre line of the motorcycle and at 0.2 m above the ground. The mean piston speed for the test shall be 13 m/sec for two-strokes and 11 m/sec for four-strokes.

For sidecar machines where the exhaust system will not permit the microphone being placed in the position stated it shall be placed in a position 45 degrees above the machine.

Drivers are required to have the stroke of engine marked on the crankcase permanently.

For International events both home and abroad, the FIM regulations will have to be met i.e. 105 dBA two-strokes, 110 dBA four-strokes.

10 Superchargers/turbochargers The use of superchargers/turbochargers is prohibited unless specifically allowed in the regulations for a specific class. An engine, whether two-stroke or four-stroke, coming within any one of the recognized classes, as determined by the capacity of the working cylinder shall not be considered as supercharged/turbocharged, when in respect of one engine cycle, the total capacity, measured geometrically, of the fuel charging device or devices, including the capacity of the engine working cylinder, if used for inspirating the fuel, does not exceed the maximum capacity of the class in question. The intracylinder injection of fuel shall not be considered as supercharging/turbocharging.

11 Handlebars The width of handlebars for motorcycles is for machines up to 80 cc not less than 400 mm. For all other machines (inc. sidecars) not less than 450 mm. Grips must be attached in such a way that at least the minimum width is reached when measured between the outside ends of the grips. Exposed handlebars must be plugged with a solid material.

The minimum angle of rotation of the handlebar on each side of the centre line or mid-position must be 20 degrees for solo motorcycles and sidecars. Whatever the position of the handlebars the front wheel must never touch the streamlining if any (see Reg. No. 18). Stops or other devices must be fitted to ensure a minimum clearance of 30 mm between handlebar with levers and the tank when on full lock to prevent trapping the driver's fingers. Handlebar clamps must be carefully radiused and engineered so as to avoid fracture points in the bar.

For all types of motorcycles, throttle controls must be self-closing when not held by hand. In all races up to and including National level a cutout device must be fitted which must be in a prominent position within easy reach of the driver and a marshal. The device must be prominently marked and may be a conventional switch or of a push-button type. If of a push type it must 'kill' the engine when pushed and not rely on the button being held down for any length of time.

12 Footrests The footrests for the driver must be placed not higher than 50 mm above a line passing through the centre of the wheels with a machine loaded and in front of a vertical line passing through the centre of the rear wheel. They must be positioned to give easy access to any control pedals.

The ends of the footrests must be rounded with a radius of not less than 8 mm. The minimum length of footrests must be not less than 10 cm (4 in.).

During a race, drivers must adopt a position with their feet on the footrests. If a driver adopts any other position he may be excluded.

13 Oil drain plugs and supply pipes All oil drain plugs must be tight and must be drilled and wired in position. Oil supply pipes must be adequately wired in position.

14 Oil catch tanks Where an oil breather pipe is fitted the outlet must discharge into a catch tank located in an easily accessible position and which must be emptied before the start of the race. It is recommended that the minimum size of catch tank shall be 250 cc for gearboxes and 500 cc for engines.

15 Petrol and oil filler caps Petrol and oil filler caps when closed must be leakproof. Additionally they must be securely locked to prevent accidental opening at any time.

16 Petrol tank breathers Non-return valves must be fitted to petrol tank breather pipes.

17 Inclination It must be possible for a motorcycle (other than a vintage machine) not being loaded, to be inclined to an angle of 50 degrees from the vertical, without any part of it other than the tyre coming in contact with the ground.

18 Streamlining The streamlining used on solo motor-cycles (Category A), must comply with the following:
(a) The front wheel, with the exception of the tyre, must be clearly visible from either side.
(b) Streamlining may project up to 50 mm in front of a vertical line drawn through the front axle.
(c) There must be no streamlining to the rear of a line drawn vertically through the axle of the rear wheel. The rim of the rear wheel must be clearly visible for the 180 degrees of its circumference to the rear of this line. No part of the machine may project to the rear of a line drawn vertically through the rearmost edge of the rim of the rear wheel.
(d) Normal mudguards are not considered as stream-lining.
(e) It must be possible to see the driver completely in the normal riding position, with the exception of the forearms, from either side, from the rear and from above.
(f) It is forbidden to use any transparent material to avoid the application of these rules.

(g) No part of the seat or saddle or anything to the rear of these must be more than 90 cm above the ground when the motorcycle is not loaded. The maximum height of the back of the rider's seat is 150 mm. This will be measured from the lowest point of the rigid base of the seat to the uppermost part of the fairing behind the rider.
(h) There must be a clearance of at least 20 mm between the streamlining and the extremities of the handlebar, or other form of steering device, including any attachments thereto, whatever the position of the handlebars. (See also Reg. No. 11.)
(i) Any part of the streamlining or windscreen which projects towards the rear of the motorcycle must be finished with rounded edges.

19 Specification of sidecars and three-wheelers in road races
Category B1 and B2
(a) The three road wheels may be disposed so as to give two or three tracks.
(b) If three tracks are made then the centres of the tracks of the motorcycle shall not be more than 75 mm apart.
(c) Wheelbase – see (e) below.
(d) The sidecar wheel may be placed either side of the motorcycle.
(e) The distance between the fore and aft centre lines of the tracks made by the motorcycle rear and sidecar wheels must be not less than 800 mm and not more than 1100 mm maximum dimensions for a B2 overall width 1700 mm (including exhaust systems).
(f) The minimum dimensions of the sidecar body shall be length 800 mm, width 300 mm (both measured 15 cm above the platform). Height of the passenger's protective screen 300 mm. Any bodywork or fairing must not pro-trude more than 400 mm in front of the most forward part of the front tyre or rearward more than 300 mm from the most rear part of the rear tyre.
(g) The engine must be positioned in front of the rear wheel in such a way that the centre line of the engine – determined by half of its overall width, overall height 600 mm at rear and 800 mm at front, overall length 3300 mm, wheelbase 2300 mm – shall not extend more than 160 mm beyond the centre line of the rear wheel track of the motorcycle. By definition the centre line of the engine is the position midway between the centre lines of outermost cylinders for transverse engines or the crankshaft for inline engines.
(h) The drive shall be transmitted to the road by the rear wheel of the motorcycle.
(i) The ground clearance of the sidecar shall be not less than 75 mm nor more than 300 mm when the machine is loaded.

The suspension of the front wheel must be designed so that under suspension action and in a straight ahead position, it shall only move vertically and in a single plane relative to the motorcycle – the plane must be in the driving direction. This must occur without changes to the camber or the side-tracking. The vertical travel of the front and rear wheel spindles under suspension action must be at least 20 mm.

The motorcycle must be steered by a non adjustable handlebar which is directly fixed to the steering unit of the motorcycle. The handlebar must not be lower than the spindle of the front wheel. The steering unit can only consist of a swinging arm or fork mounted on a single or double stanchion or a telescopic fork. The steering unit must operate through the front wheel without any intermediate articulated steering joints fitted.

(j) The provision of coachwork or streamlining is optional, but the vehicle must have accommodation for a passenger and the coachwork or streamlining shall not impede complete freedom of movement by the driver or passenger at all times. No part of the seat or saddle or anything to the rear of these must be more than 600 mm above the ground when the motorcycle is not loaded.

(k) A passenger must be carried and must always be protected from the road wheels and both primary and final drives either by mudguard or some other means.

(l) There shall be a clearance of at least 20 mm between the streamlining and the extremities of the handlebar, including any attachments thereto whatever the position of the handlebar (see also Reg. No. 11).

(m) Where batteries are located in the sidecar nose they must be adequately wrapped to prevent injury to passengers in the event of acid discharge.

(n) A solid and effective protection between the driver and the engine must prevent direct contact between his body or clothes and/or escaping flames or leaking fuel and oil.

(o) A cutout device must be fitted which must be in a prominent position within easy reach of the driver and a marshal. The device must be prominently marked and may be a conventional switch or of a push-button type. If of a push type it must 'kill' the engine when pushed and not rely on the button being held down for any length of time. This applies up to and including National level only. FOR INTERNATIONAL EVENTS FIM RULES APPLY WHICH REQUIRES THE USE OF LANYARDS.

(p) Any electric fuel feed pump must be wired in such a way as to cut out if the engine 'kill' device is operated as in 19(o).

NOTE – Vintage machines without batteries are exempt from the requirements of (o) and (p) above.

20 Streamlining (Categories B1, B2 and B3) The streamlining on three-wheelers must be designed and fitted to allow complete liberty of movement to the driver, both when driving and when getting on or off the vehicle, without the streamlining or any part of it having to be displaced.

For B2 sidecars neither the driver nor the passenger must be covered from above nor may they be attached in any way. Furthermore, the passenger must be able to lean out on either side. Spoilers and other aerodynamic devices must not surpass the streamlining. The streamlining must not have any sharp edges.

The extreme forward part of the streamlining must not project forward in plan beyond the most forward part of the front tyre by more than 400 mm.

The height above the ground of the rear part of the streamlining and of any part of the saddle or any other component of the motorcycle shall not exceed 600 mm when the motorcycle is not loaded.

There shall be a clearance of at least 20 mm between the streamlining and the extremities of the handlebar (or other form of steering lever), including any attachment thereto whatever the position of the handlebar. (See also Reg. No. 11.) The streamlining must be securely fixed front and rear, but if the front of the streamlining drops it must not be possible for the front wheel to over-run the streamlining.

21 Fuel For all road races the fuel must be commercial fuel, that is to say as sold at roadside service stations for licenced vehicles in that country or available from other local sources for use in aircraft used by commercial airlines (aviation gasolene).

POWER BOOSTERS AND OCTANE BOOSTERS ARE STRICTLY FORBIDDEN.

Samples of fuel for the purpose of testing may be taken from the tank of any motorcycle which takes part in the competition.

22 Number plates Whenever number plates are required to be carried at an event they will be three in number and must comply with the following requirements. They must be made of rigid material and solidly constructed, measuring a minimum of 235 × 285 mm in size. The number plates will be rectangular with 50 mm radius rounded corners, the minimum measurements will remain unchanged. The plates must be flat or slightly curved (not more than 1 in. from the true plane) and must not be otherwise bent or obscured in any way. One plate must be carried facing forward and not more than 25 degrees from the vertical and others must be facing outwards and vertical, one on each side of the machine.

The minimum dimensions of the figures must be: height 140 mm, width 90 mm, width of stroke 25 mm, and the space between any two figures 25 mm.

The figures must be legible and both figures and background must be in a 'matt' (non-shiny) colour.

The colours shall be as follows.

Front and Side Plates
Solo motorcycles up to 80 cc – white plates with black numbers
Over 100 cc to 125 cc – black plates with white numbers
Over 125 cc to 250 cc – green plates with white numbers
Over 250 cc to 350 cc – blue plates with white numbers

Over 350 cc to 500 cc – yellow plates with black numbers
Over 500 cc to 750 cc – white plates with black numbers
Over 750 cc to 1300 cc – red plates with white numbers
TT Formula I – white plates with black numbers
TT Formula II – black plates with white numbers
Three-wheelers – white plates with black numbers
Three-wheelers (FII Sidecars) – red plates with white numbers.

They must be so fixed that they are clearly visible and not obscured by any part of the machine or by the driver when he is in the riding position.

In place of detachable plates similar areas may be painted on the body of the machine or on the streamlining.

Where yellow, green or blue are required the colours shall comply with BS 4800: 1972 as follows: Yellow 10E53; Green 14E53; Blue 18E53.

Any other number plate or any marking on the motorcycle that might be confused with a number plate must be removed before the driver is allowed to start.

23 Helmets Helmets bearing the gold ACU stamp and in a sound condition and properly fitted, must be worn by all drivers and passengers while practising and racing. Only helmets providing full protection to the temples will be permitted. Helmets not meeting ACU requirements may be impounded by the chief scrutineer for the duration of the meeting.

24 Protective clothing In all practising and racing, leather protective clothing in a sound condition, including gloves and boots, must be worn by every driver and passenger. Two-piece riding leathers will only be acceptable if fully zipped together.

For drivers, the boots must be leather and calf length or of such length as to ensure that the legs are completely covered in leather, i.e. riding leathers must be properly tucked into the boots so that no gaps can appear. Short ankle boots and boots with metal studs are not permissible.

Passengers may wear any type of footwear of a durable material which must be non skid.

Goggles or visors and spectacles, if worn, must be of non-splinterable material, abrasion resistant material marked to British Standard BS 4110-ZA.

25 Identification discs While practising and racing drivers and passengers are required to wear an identification disc around the neck, attached by a material approved by the scrutineer. The disc must be permanently marked with the wearer's full name and date of birth and preferably the blood group.

It is recommended that identification discs shall be of a durable material, circular in shape, between 20 mm and 25 mm in diameter and having rounded edges with no sharp or ragged projections.

26 Method of starting Unless otherwise stated in the Supplementary Regulations, all races will be by mass start, with dead engines. Drivers will take up their positions on the grid. The method of allocating such positions shall be stated in the Supplementary Regulations.

The number of starters will be as laid down in the track permit. For a staggered start an additional 25% of starters may be included as long as there are no more than three classes and a time gap equivalent to 1/3 of a lap is allowed between each class, for practice an additional 50% of riders may be included unless otherwise stated in the track permit.

All solo and sidecar machines shall be started by the driver and/or the passenger unaided except where the permission of the Clerk of the Course has been granted. Where a pusher is authorized for a solo machine, there will be a 5-second delay, following the mass start, before the pusher is allowed to assist. Cycle-cars will start from the rear row of the grid with the driver seated. One pusher, in addition to the passenger, will be allowed for a distance of 30 yards. Immediately the machine starts or reaches the 30 yards line, the pusher must leave the course on his nearest side and return to the paddock. Mechanical starting devices may be fitted but must not be used for the initial start of a race unless stated otherwise in the Supplementary Regulations.

27 Start procedure
(a) Drivers to proceed to grid positions as directed.
(b) Proceed on warming up lap(s) as indicated. When the drivers reach the grid after this lap(s) change of machine is forbidden. An Official of the Meeting will display as quickly as possible:
(c) The 3-minute countdown board. All persons other than drivers or officials must evacuate the grid area. All engines must be stopped. Display of helmet panel requesting all drivers to check that their helmet strap is securely fastened.
(d) The 1-minute countdown board will be displayed.
(e) The 30-second countdown board will be displayed.
(f) The signal indicating the start of the race either by lights changing from red to green or national flag. (Note: any driver moving when red light is displayed or flag raised may be penalized).
(g) In the event of adverse weather conditions, the clerk of the course may delay the start by a **maximum** of 10 minutes after the completion of the warming-up lap.

28 Starter's orders Only those drivers in the starting area or on a grid will be deemed to be under starter's orders. No other driver will be permitted to start in a race.

29 False start A false start occurs when, before the signal to start is given, a driver moves forward from his prescribed position. The driver concerned may be penalized by the addition of up to one minute to his total time for the race.

30 Flag signals The following code of flag signals will be used where appropriate:

National flag (lowered) or green signal light = Start.

Red = Immediate stop all drivers.

Black with driver's number = That driver stop.

Yellow (waved) = Slow down, driver must be prepared to stop. OVERTAKING STRICTLY FORBIDDEN.*

Yellow (motionless) = Signal of danger.

Green = Course clear.

White flag, with or without red cross = Slow moving intervention vehicle on track.

Red flag with three yellow vertical bands = Deterioration of adhesion of the track.

Yellow flag and red flag with yellow bands crossed = Race stopped by the clerk of the course.

Yellow flag with black diagonal cross = Start of last lap.

Chequered black and white = Finish.

Any additional flag signals will be stated in the Supplementary Regulations.

Only authorized officials are permitted to use these flags. All the above flags should measure not less than 750 × 600 mm.

* Any driver judged to have taken advantage whilst the WAVED yellow flag was displayed will be considered guilty of unfair and/or dangerous driving and will be excluded.

31 Finish of race The chequered flag will be displayed as the winner crosses the finishing line and will be kept flying thereafter until the last driver finishes that lap.

No driver will be allowed to start a fresh lap after the chequered flag has been displayed. Thereafter drivers crossing the line will be flagged off, their position being determined by the number of laps each has completed, those drivers who complete a similar number of laps having their position determined by the order in which they finish. Only drivers crossing the finishing line within the time limit and/or distance laid down in the Supplementary Regulations will be declared finishers.

32 Stopping and restarting a race

32.1 Should it be necessary to stop the race due to an incident or if climatic or other conditions make it hazardous to continue, a red flag signal will be given at the start/finish line and simultaneously a signal comprising of the yellow flag crossed with the red flag with yellow bands will be given at all flag marshals' posts to indicate that the race has been stopped.

32.2 The decision to stop the race can only come from the clerk of the course or, in circumstances outside his control by the next in command as indicated in the programme.

32.3 When these signals have been given, each driver must immediately stop racing, slow down and return to the starting area, knowing that his placing will be determined by his position in the race when he last crossed the finishing line.

32.4 The conditions under which a race will be restarted are as follows:

32.4.1 *If two laps or less have been completed by the race leader.* The original start shall be declared null and void. All riders taking part in the original start shall be allowed to restart either on their original machine or on a machine of the same make provided it has been approved as fit to race by the scrutineers. The restarted race shall be for the full race distance and the original grid positions will be used. The place of any motorcycle unable to take part in the restart shall be left vacant. If it is impossible to restart the race, no points will be awarded towards any championships involved.

32.4.2 *If more than 2 laps but less than 75% of the race distance have been completed by the leader.*

(a) The race shall be considered to be in two parts. The race positions at the end of the first part will be calculated in accordance with paragraph 32.3 above.

(b) The distance of the restarted race will be that required to make up the initial full race distance.

(c) The grid for the restart will be in the order, given by the chief timekeeper, of the machines at the end of the first part.

(d) Only those machines which took part in the original start and which have not been withdrawn from the race and which return to the starting area by an authorized route and without any unauthorized assistance may restart. Machines may be repaired.

(e) When the race is run in two parts, the final classification will be based on the addition of the two times for riders having the same number of laps.

(f) In cases where the races are of short duration, the meeting is of lower than National status and there are not sufficient timekeepers available to implement these provisions, the clerk of the course is permitted to re-run the race over a distance appropriate to the conditions.

(g) If it is impossible to restart the race, half points will be awarded towards any championship involved.

32.4.3 *If more than 75% of the full race distance has been completed by the leader.*

(a) This shall be declared a full race.

(b) The classification will be calculated in accordance with paragraph 32.3 above.

(c) Only those drivers and machines which have not been withdrawn from the race and which return to the starting area by an authorized route and without unauthorized assistance will be included in the results.

(d) Full championship points will be awarded where applicable.

32.5 Should the end of the race signal inadvertently or otherwise be displayed before the leading driver completes the scheduled number of laps – or before the prescribed race time has been completed – the race will nevertheless be deemed to end at the moment the signal is given. Should the end of the race signal be inadvertently delayed, the race will nevertheless be deemed to finish at the correct moment and competitors be classified accordingly.

33 Outside assistance If, during a race, a driver receives outside assistance, other than that provided by the organizers for the removal of himself or his machine from the course in the interests of safety, he will be excluded.

34 Foul, unfair or dangerous driving The clerk of the course shall exclude immediately any driver who is in his opinion guilty of any foul, unfair or dangerous driving, either in the practice or in the actual race.

35 Course conduct During a competition, driver and passengers shall not indulge in any foul, unfair or dangerous practice.

It is forbidden, without exception, to drive or wheel a machine in the reverse direction of racing.

Competitors passing or being passed must not hinder other competitors.

If, for any reason, a driver leaves the course, he must rejoin without any outside assistance and, if possible, at the point at which he left the course. He must not gain any advantage, if any advantage is attained he will be excluded from the results, alternatively he must retire. All due consideration must be given/must be taken, at all times.

It is absolutely forbidden to leave a motorcycle near a bend. In cases where a competitor requires first aid, it is permitted for him to travel on foot in the reverse direction of racing provided he exercises due care to avoid any danger to other competitors.

It is absolutely forbidden for a driver on a solo machine to carry any other person.

Repairs to motorcycles carried out on the course must be effected only with any such tools as are carried on the machine or by the competitor.

All competitors who retire during a race must leave the course with their motorcycle at the very first available opportunity, at all times ensuring that they do not place themselves or their machines in such a position as to constitute a danger to other competitors.

The penalty for breaking these rules may be exclusion.

36 Alterations to programme In the event of a race being cancelled due to insufficient entries, the promoters reserve the right to offer the race time and prizes for a race of similar length for machines of another class or category.

37 Scrutineering/machine examination The scrutineer/machine examiner shall check both the machine and the rider for compliance with the regulations enforced for the discipline concerned and for the Road Traffic Act if applicable. Where specifications are set down in respect of clothing, helmets etc. the rider must wear his clothing prior to scrutineering to demonstrate good fit etc.

Appendix 3: Clothing

ACU approved protective helmets and visors

Helmets bearing any one of the undermentioned 'standard' marks may be approved by the ACU if deemed to conform with certain additional criteria considered necessary for helmets used in motorcycle sport. Helmets so approved will carry the ACU transfer in gold or silver.

British Standards Institution – BS 2495 amend. 5.
British Standards Institution – BS 5361 amend. 5.
British Standards Institution – BS 6658–A.
British Standards Institution – BS 6658–B.
Snell Memorial Institute – Snell 85.

Please note the only indication that a helmet is suitable for immediate use in motorcycle sport is the ACU gold or silver stamp firmly affixed. It is considered that any person selling a helmet for competition use as 'ACU Approved' without an approval stamp firmly affixed is making a false trade description.

Gold Approval
The minimum standard for Road Racing, Sprints, Drag Racing, Hillclimb and any other event held wholly on metalled surfaces.

Silver Approval
The minimum standard for Moto Cross, Grass Track, Enduro, Speedway, Grass Hill Climb and all 'Off Road' speed events.

White Approval
Only permitted for use in non speed events.

Helmet security

Many helmets have a type of buckle (Double 'D' Ring or Sliding Bar) requiring strap tension to maintain security. Riders should be aware that strap slip can occur through this type of buckle even on new helmets, be sure to maintain some strap tension at all times.

Even during the relatively short period of a race, strap slip can be sufficient to increase the risk of helmet loss in the event of an accident. It can be minimized by securing the flapping strap end by some means such as a rubber band.

From 1 January 1989 Gold Approval will only be granted to harness retained helmets if they are fitted with a positive quick release seatbelt-type fastener, approved by the British Standards Institution.

Helmet stamping

Helmets which are to be mailed for approval and stamping should be sent to:

Auto Cycle Union
Miller House
Corporation Street
Rugby
Warwickshire
CV21 2DN
Tel: 0788 540519

A fee of £4.00 should also be enclosed which covers return post and packing charges.

Helmets may also be stamped for personal callers by some members of the Technical Committee. Please contact the Technical Secretary at headquarters for details of the nearest authorized member.

Scrutineering of helmets

The Chief Scrutineer of an event has the power to impound for the day, any helmet he considers is not in a fit condition to be used. He is authorized to remove the ACU approval sticker, which remains the property of the Auto Cycle Union. The helmet may be submitted for a second opinion to the Technical Secretary, but in any case may not be used without being rechecked.

The Union recommends that all types of helmets used in regular competition should be replaced after two years.

Moulded plastic helmets

Many helmets with moulded plastic shells of thermo plastic material meet with ACU requirements and bear the Union's mark of approval. However, it must be stressed that helmets manufactured from this material can be seriously damaged by substances such as petrol, paint, adhesives, cleaning agents and decorative stickers.

Visors/goggles

For Road Racing, visors to the highest British Standards Institution grade of impact and abrasion resistance are required – BS 4110-ZA. (Laminated glass accepted).

Ten fitting tests for helmets

1 Obtain correct size by measuring the crown of the head.
2 Check there is no side to side movement.
3 Tighten strap securely.
4 With head forward attempt to pull up back of helmet to ensure helmet cannot be removed in this way.
5 Check ability to see clearly over shoulder.
6 Make sure nothing impedes your breathing in the helmet and never cover nose or mouth.
7 Never wind a scarf around neck so that air is stopped from entering the helmet. Never wear scarf under the retention strap.
8 Ensure that visor can be opened with one gloved hand.
9 Satisfy yourself that the back of your helmet is designed to protect your neck.
10 Always buy the best you can afford.

Make sure that the helmet has an ACU Approval Stamp affixed.

Never buy from mail-order unless you are satisfied with the above tests. Do not be afraid to return the helmet unused if it does not fit you.

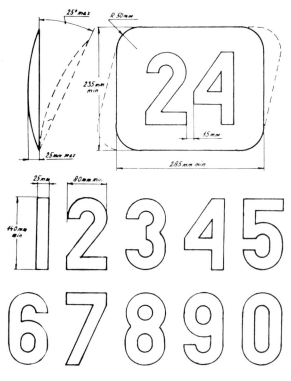

Dimensions of numbers and plates

Other motorcycle titles from Osprey

Osprey Collector's Library

AJS and Matchless – The Postwar Models
Roy Bacon   0 85045 536 7

Ariel – The Postwar Models
Roy Bacon   0 85045 537 5

BMW Twins & Singles
Roy Bacon   0 85045 699 1

British Motorcycles of the 1930s
Roy Bacon   0 85045 657 6

British Motorcycles of the 1960s
Roy Bacon   0 85045 785 8

BSA Gold Star and Other Singles
Roy Bacon   0 85045 447 6

BSA Twins & Triples
Roy Bacon   0 85045 368 2

Classic British Scramblers
Don Morley   0 85045 649 5

Classic British Trials Bikes
Don Morley   0 85045 545 6

Classic British Two-Stroke Trials Bikes
Don Morley   0 85045 745 9

Classic Motorcycle Racer Tests
Alan Cathcart   0 85045 589 8

Ducati Singles
Mick Walker   0 85045 605 3

Ducati Twins
Mick Walker   0 85045 634 7

Gilera Road Racers
Raymond Ainscoe   0 85045 675 4

Greeves
Rob Carrick and Mick Walker
0 85045 882 X

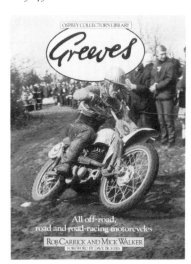

Honda – The Early Classic Motorcycles
Roy Bacon   0 85045 596 0

Moto Guzzi Singles
Mick Walker   0 85045 712 2

Moto Guzzi Twins
Mick Walker   0 85045 650 9

MV Agusta
Mick Walker   0 85045 711 4

Norton Singles
Roy Bacon   0 85045 485 9

Norton Twins
Roy Bacon   0 85045 423 9

Royal Enfield – The Postwar Models
Roy Bacon   0 85045 459 X

Spanish Post-war Road and Racing Motorcycles
Mick Walker   0 85045 705 X

Spanish Trials Bikes
Don Morley   0 85045 663 0

Suzuki Two-Strokes
Roy Bacon   0 85045 588 X

Triumph Twins & Triples
Roy Bacon   0 85045 700 9

Velocette Flat Twins
Roy Bacon   0 85045 632 0

Villiers Singles & Twins
Roy Bacon   0 85045 486 7

Vincent Vee Twins
Roy Harper   0 85045 435 2

Yamaha Dirtbikes
Colin MacKellar   0 85045 660 6

Yamaha Two-Stroke Twins
Colin MacKellar   0 85045 582 0

Osprey Colour Series

Fast Bikes
Colin Schiller   0 85045 761 0

Japanese 100 hp/11 sec/150 mph Motorcycles
Tim Parker   0 85045 647 9

Road Racers Revealed
Alan Cathcart   0 85045 762 9

Restoration Series

BSA Singles Restoration
Roy Bacon   0 85045 709 2

BSA Twin Restoration
Roy Bacon   0 85045 699 X

Norton Twin Restoration
Roy Bacon   0 85045 708 4

Triumph Twin Restoration
Roy Bacon   0 85045 635 5

Restoring Motorcycles

1 Four-Stroke Engines
Roy Bacon   0 85045 787 4

2 Electrics
Roy Bacon   0 85045 788 2

3 Transmissions
Roy Bacon   0 85045 859 5

4 Two-Stroke Engines
Roy Bacon   0 85045 860 9

General

Ducati Motorcycles
Alan Cathcart   0 85045 510 3

Ducati – The Untold Story
Alan Cathcart   0 85045 789 0

Geoff Duke
In Pursuit of Perfection
Geoff Duke   0 85045 838 2

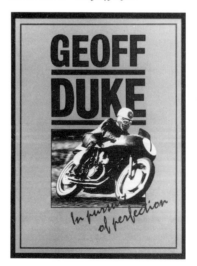

German Motorcycles
Mick Walker   0 85045 759 9

Honda Gold Wing
Peter Rae   0 85045 567 7

Motorcycle Chassis Design: the theory and practice
Tony Foale and Vic Willoughby
0 85045 560 X

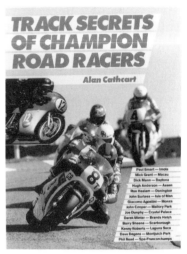

Track Secrets of Champion Road Racers
Alan Cathcart   0 85045 774 2

Write for a free catalogue of motorcycle books to:
The Sales Manager
Osprey Publishing Limited
59 Grosvenor Street
London W1X 9DA